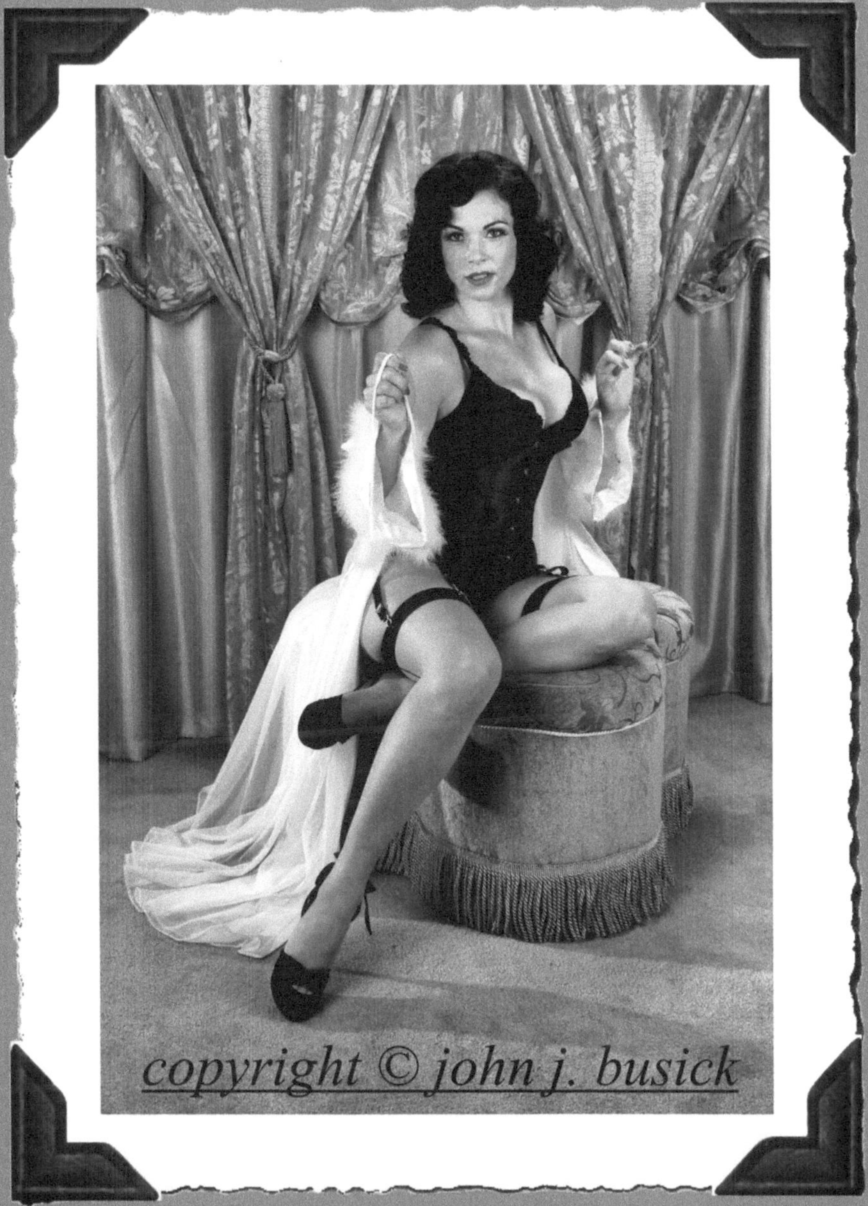

Model: Veronica Wyles | Photo: John J. Busick of Riverview Photographic Studio | MUAH Kristine Falsetta

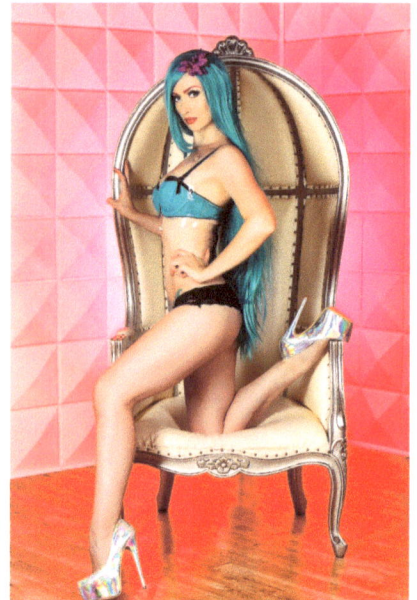

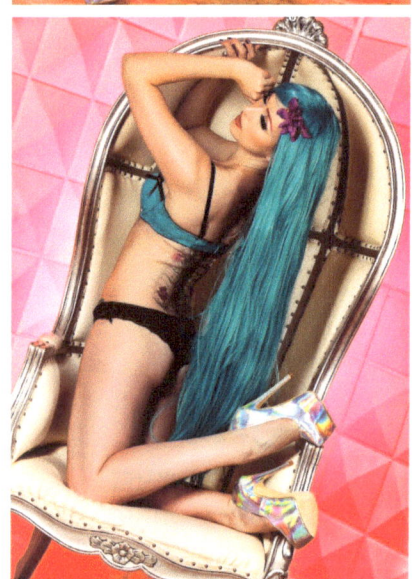

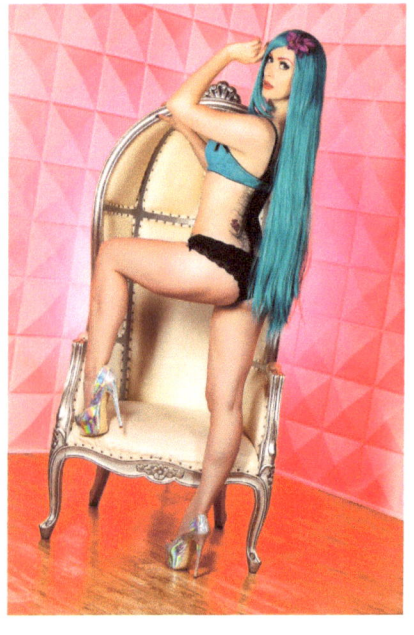

NEA DUNE

Photos | Quantography

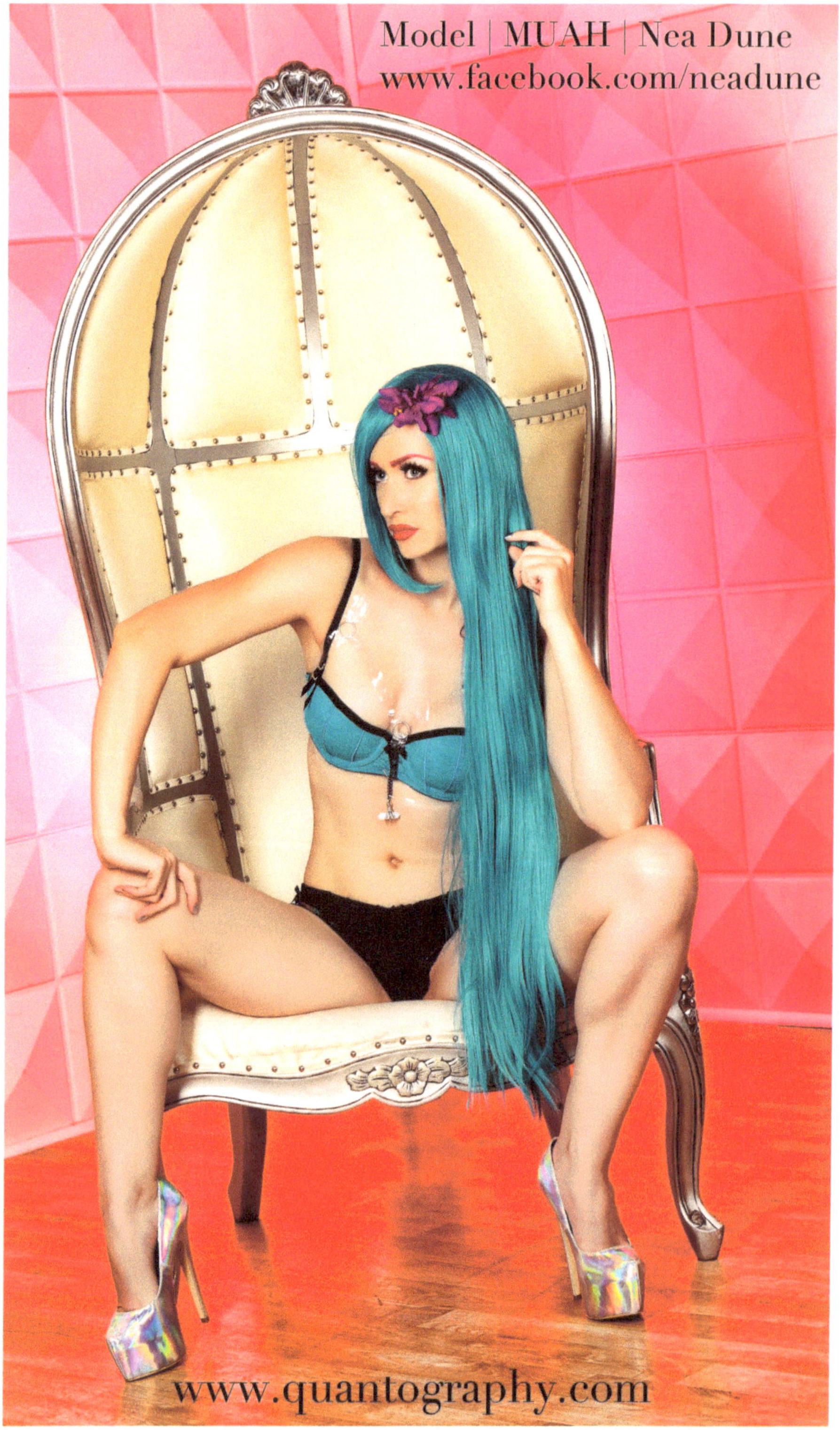

Model | MUAH | Nea Dune
www.facebook.com/neadune

www.quantography.com

PINUP ALTERNATIVE
www.PinupAlternativeMagazine.com

Follow Us (but not in a creepy way)
www.facebook.com/pinupalternativemagazine
Instagram @pinupalternative
Twitter @pinupaltmag
Submit to: PinupAlternativeMagazine@gmail.com

Issue 1 February 2015

Veronica Wyles *"Tomboy Turned Pinup"*

**Photos by John J. Busick
of Riverview Photographic Studio
Makeup Artist | Kristine Falsetta**

"When you find something that fits it feels good. That is how I feel about discovering the Pinup look and style," says New York based Pin-Up Model, Veronica Wyles, who started off as a self described Tomboy. After discovering Pinup Culture and fashion she quickly became adapted to her new sexy skin. As Veronica says, *"It fits me perfectly. As I continue my journey in the modeling world I have found that I am a chameleon and have the ability to take on any era or style that is needed."*

Veronica's fun and outgoing personality has won her an extremely loyal fan base on social media such as Facebook and Instagram, which is where I first learned about her. Veronica always takes the time to address her fans and is funny, outgoing and humble. Veronica says, *"As a former tomboy I do not wear a princess crown nor pretend to be above anyone or anything."*

In addition to her modeling work Veronica recently became the brand embassador of specialty plus size bra store, Helen of Troy Bras. Having first hand experience in the trials and tribulations of finding a perfect fit for her ample bossom, Veronica is more than qualified to answer any questions customers might have about finding the proper bra size and style for themselves.

Veronica is also a single Mom, and from what I have seen, she seems like the most fun mom in the world. If you want to win Veronica's heart you better have a great sense of humor and an unlimited supply of dark chocolate.

Follow Veronica Wyles:
www.VeronicaWyles.com
IG @veronicawyles
facebook.com/
VeronicaMaeWyles

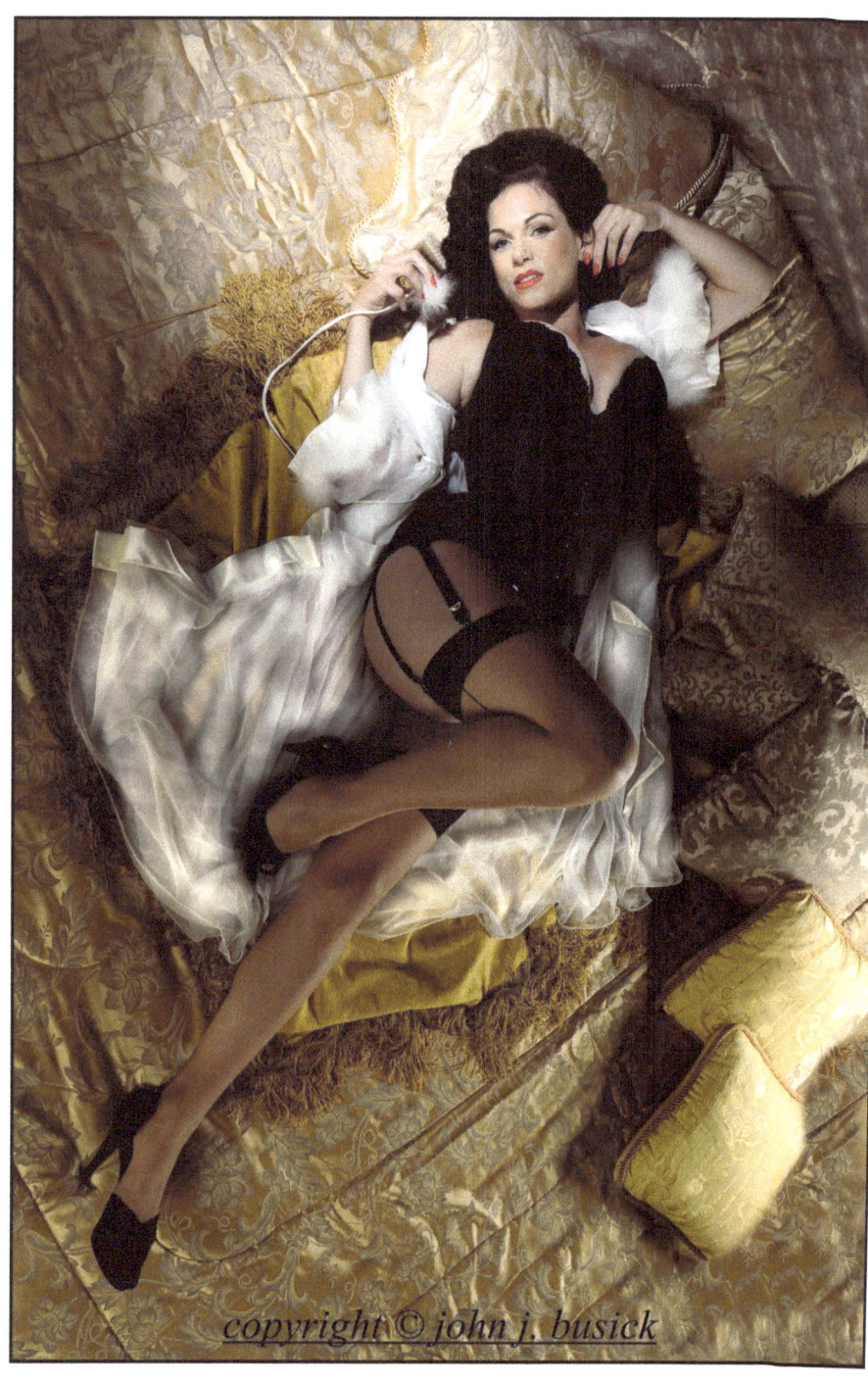

copyright © john j. busick

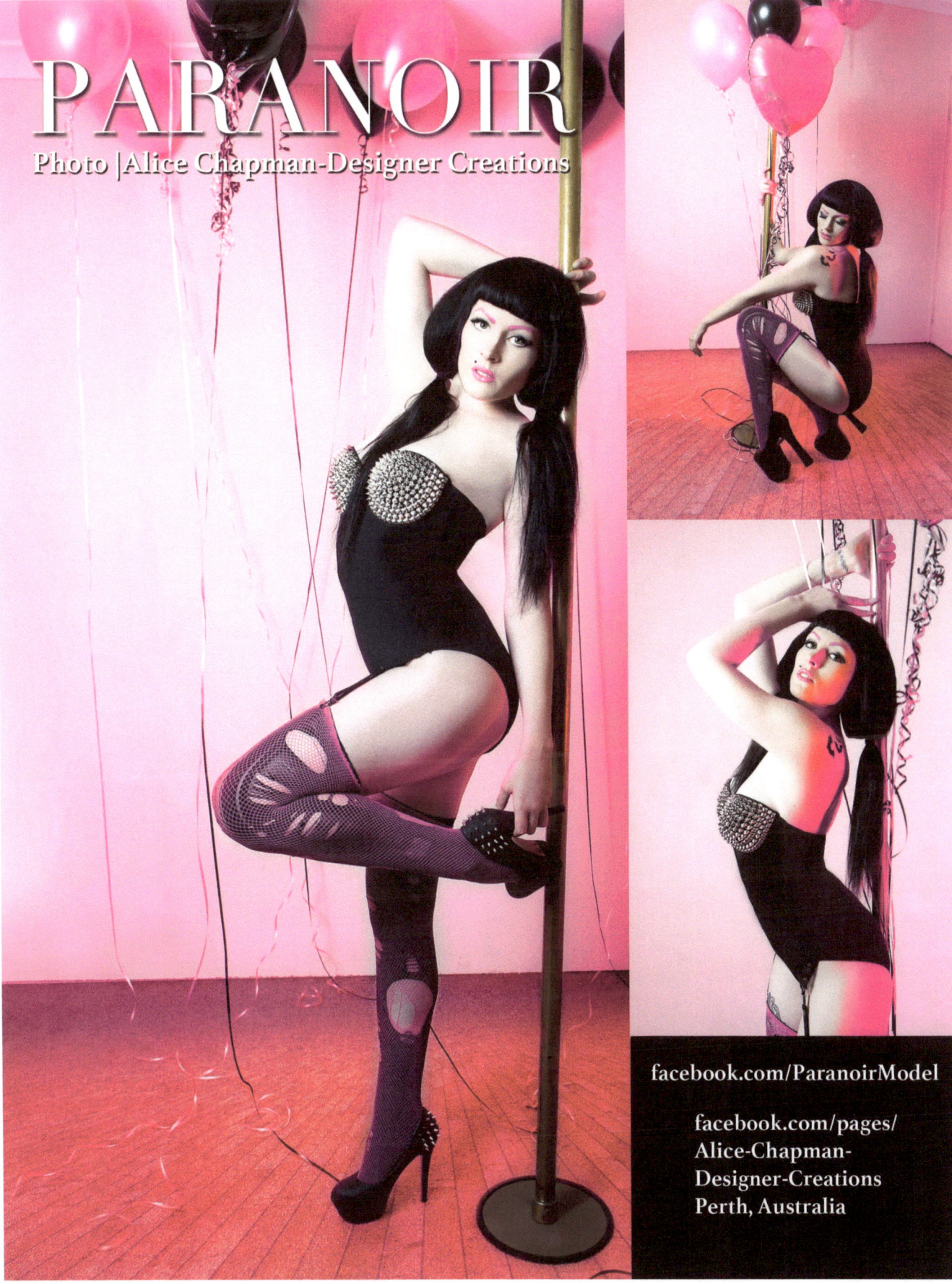

PARANOIR

Photo |Alice Chapman-Designer Creations

facebook.com/ParanoirModel

facebook.com/pages/
Alice-Chapman-
Designer-Creations
Perth, Australia

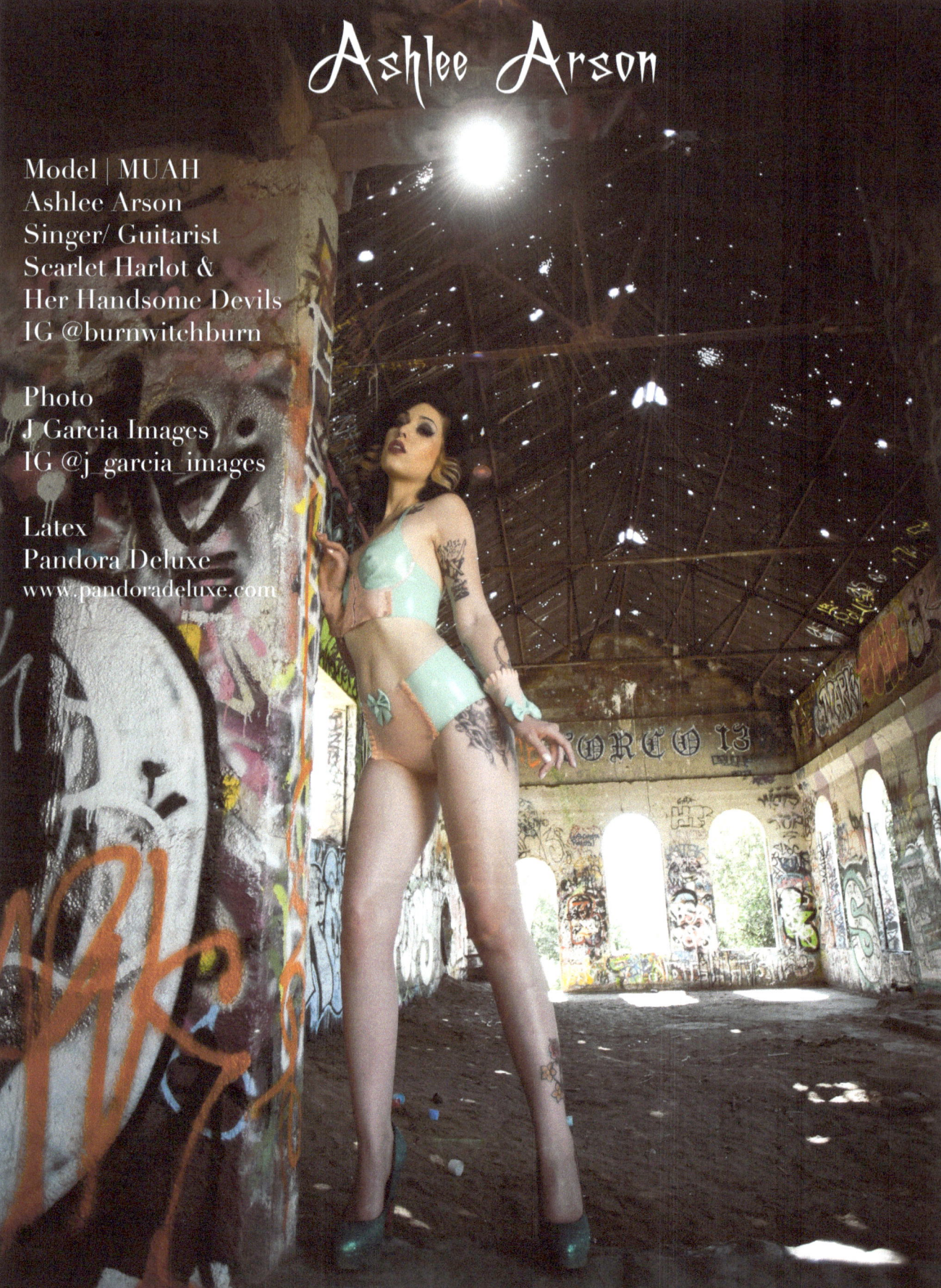

Ashlee Arson

Model | MUAH
Ashlee Arson
Singer/ Guitarist
Scarlet Harlot &
Her Handsome Devils
IG @burnwitchburn

Photo
J Garcia Images
IG @j_garcia_images

Latex
Pandora Deluxe
www.pandoradeluxe.com

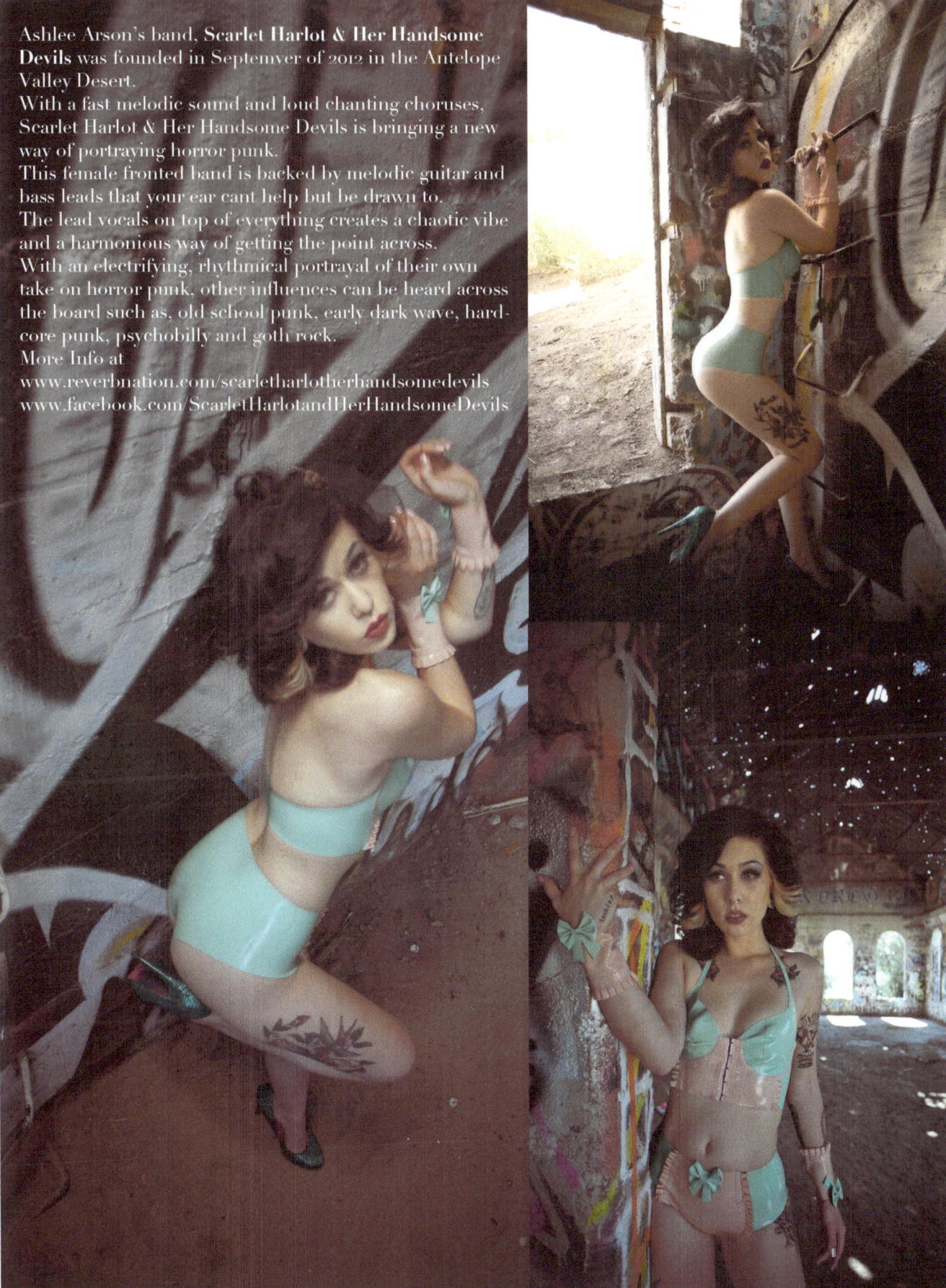

Ashlee Arson's band, **Scarlet Harlot & Her Handsome Devils** was founded in Septemver of 2012 in the Antelope Valley Desert.

With a fast melodic sound and loud chanting choruses, Scarlet Harlot & Her Handsome Devils is bringing a new way of portraying horror punk.

This female fronted band is backed by melodic guitar and bass leads that your ear cant help but be drawn to.

The lead vocals on top of everything creates a chaotic vibe and a harmonious way of getting the point across.

With an electrifying, rhythmical portrayal of their own take on horror punk, other influences can be heard across the board such as, old school punk, early dark wave, hardcore punk, psychobilly and goth rock.

More Info at
www.reverbnation.com/scarletharlotherhandsomedevils
www.facebook.com/ScarletHarlotandHerHandsomeDevils

BO VIXXEN

"Mermaid Tales"

Model | Bo Vixxen

Photo | Gina Barbara Photogaphy

Hair | Beauty by Marlene Campos

Tail | Mertailor

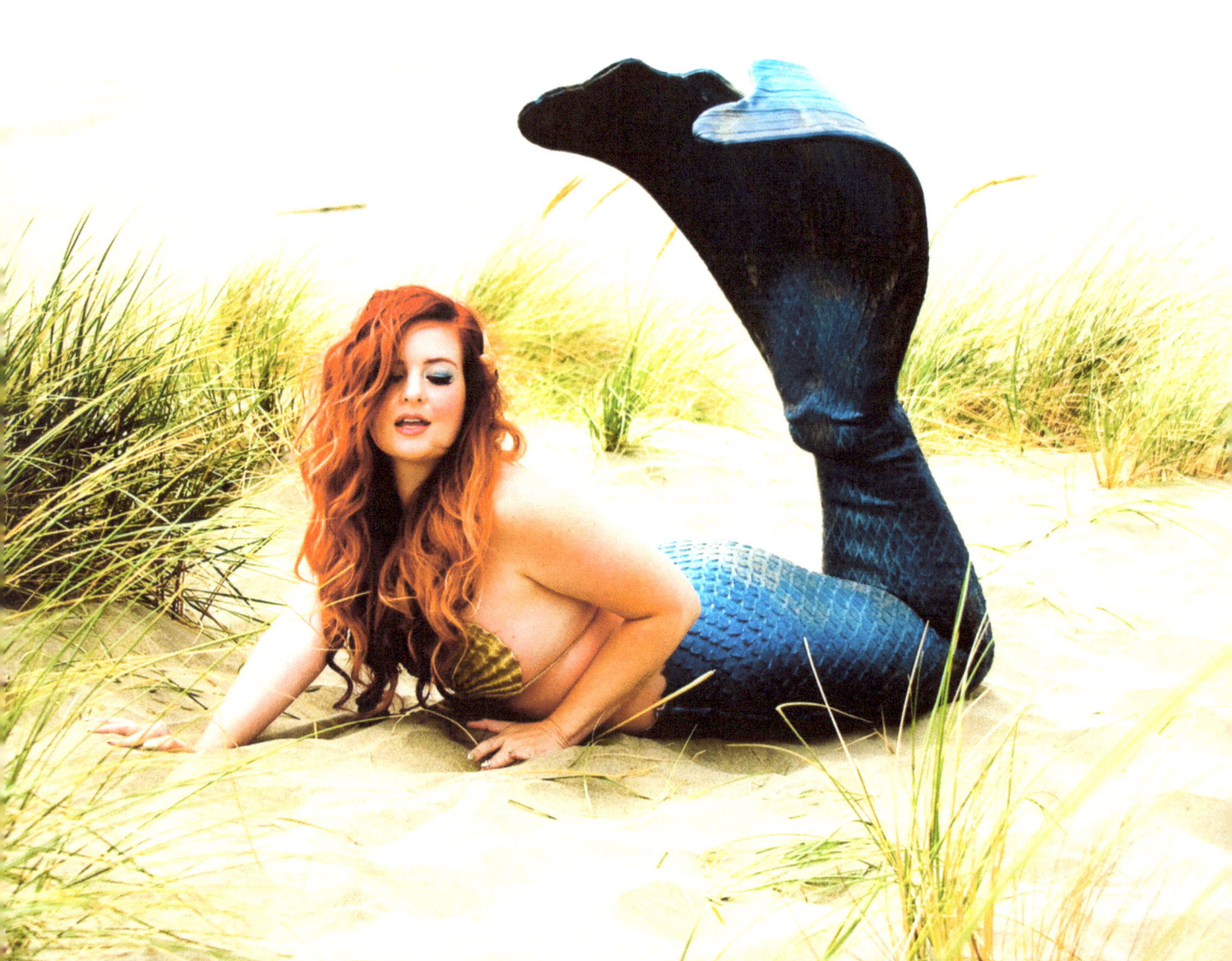

Bo Vixxen is a Disney character, actress, song bird, burlesque performer, model and a real life mermaid! She is currently based in the San Francisco Bay area and can be seen performing with the Hubba Hubba Review burlesque troop.

Instagram @bovixxen
facebook.com/bo.mermaid.vixxen

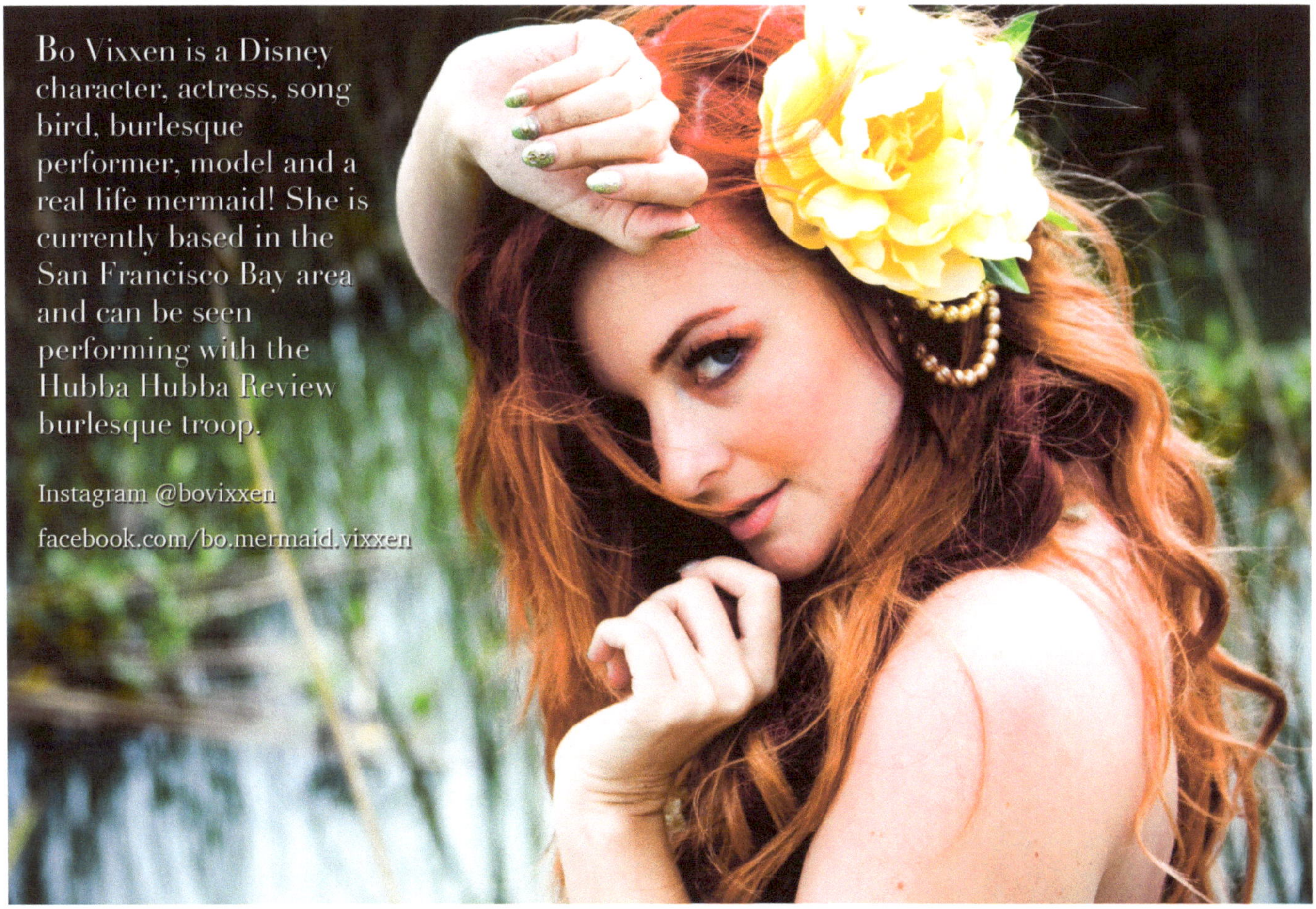

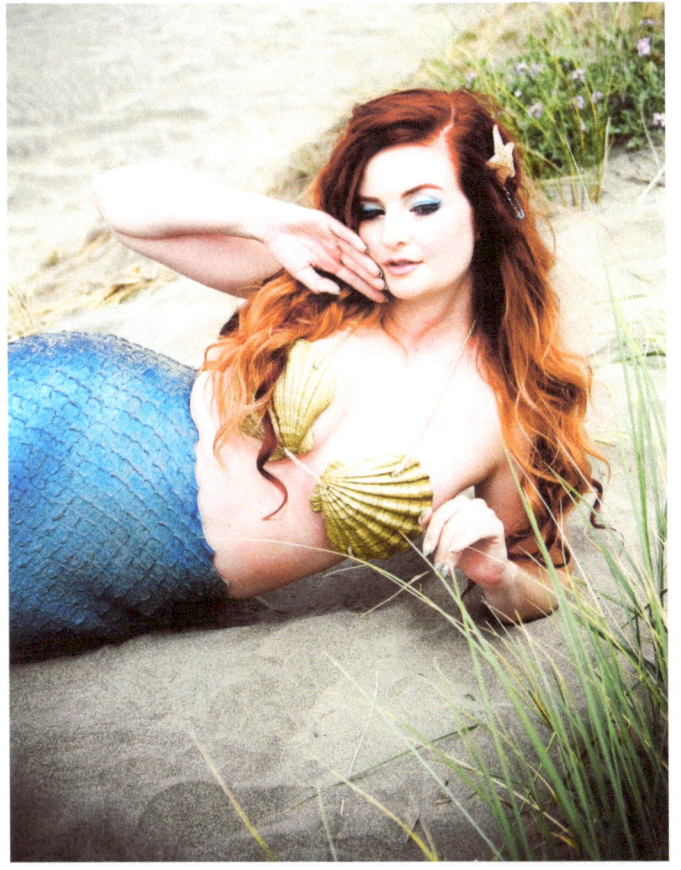
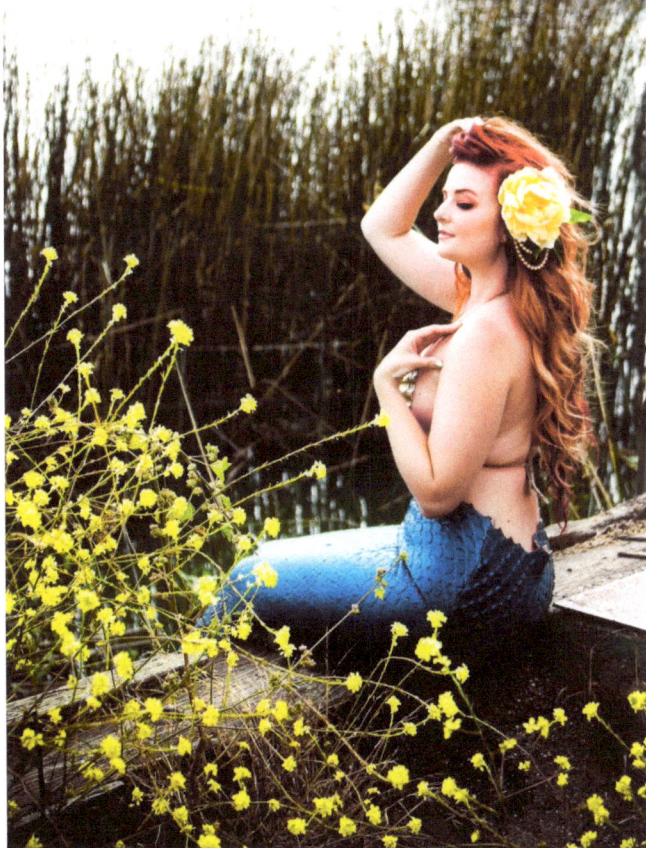

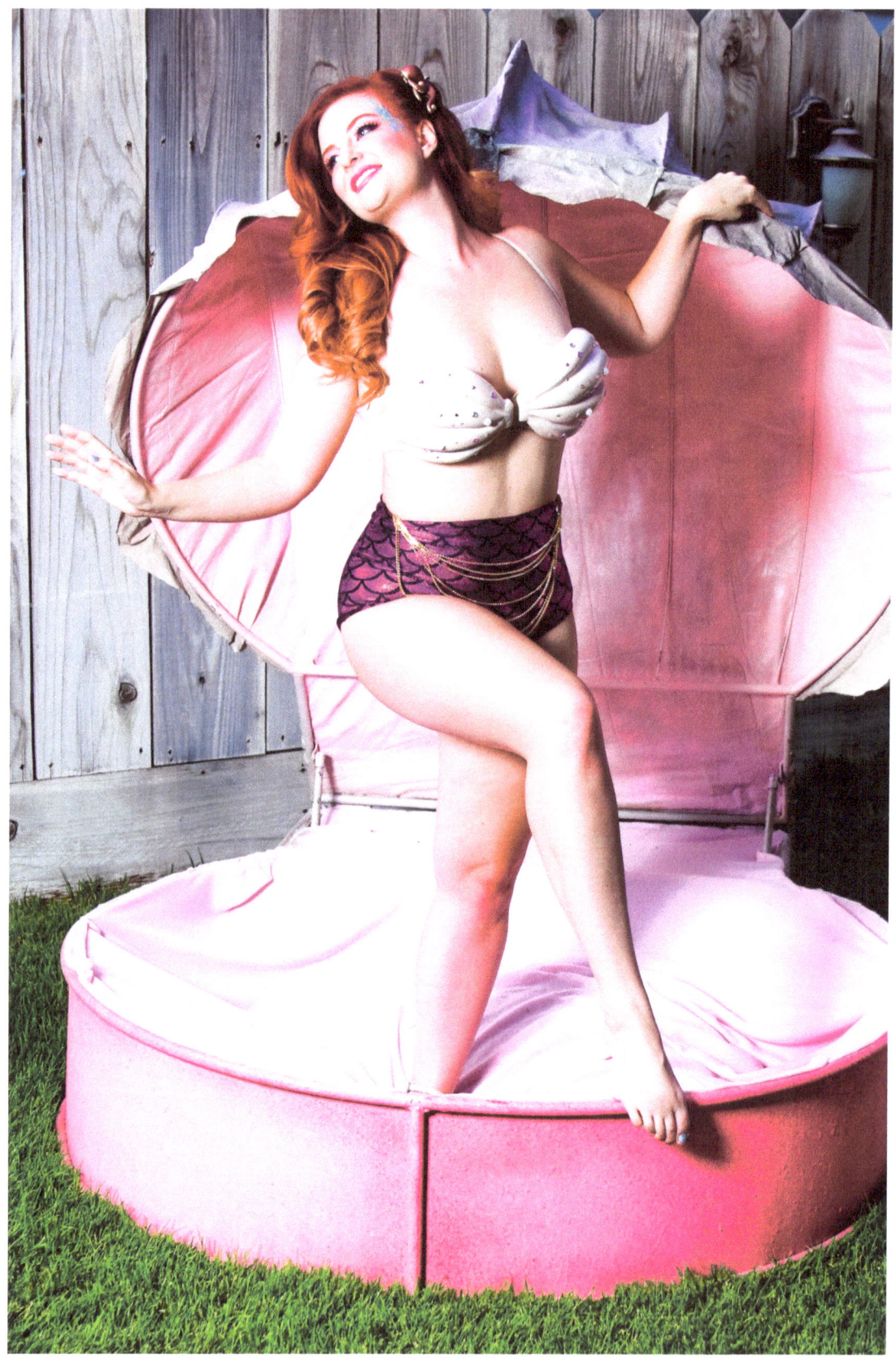

Photo | Gina Barbara Photography
Bikini Bottom | Shopoholic
Clam Shell | Hourglass Photography

Gina Barbara is a published fashion, fetish, and pin up photographer based out of her hometown of San Francisco. She has always been a strong artistic individual. In this photo collaboration with designer Firefly Path, she makes the fantasy of being a mermaid a reality with the gorgeous model Bo Vixxen.

Gina's photo style is feminine, flirty, and just plain fun. Every color is extra saturated, every line perfectly crisp, and every model leaves the shoot feeling like a star. She loves building relationships with artistically driven women who are interested in helping one another achieve their dreams. Gina Barbara is constantly striving to make women's fairytale visions come true, even if only in a photo.

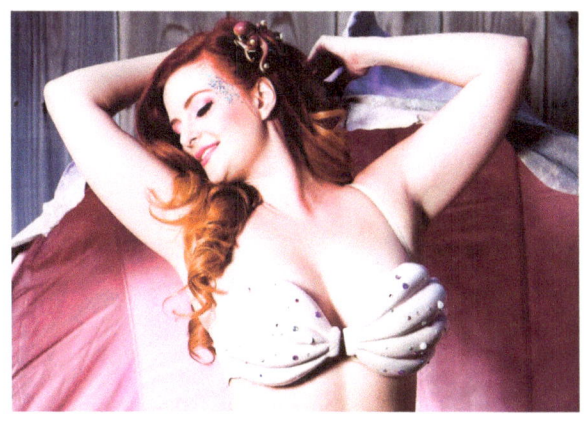

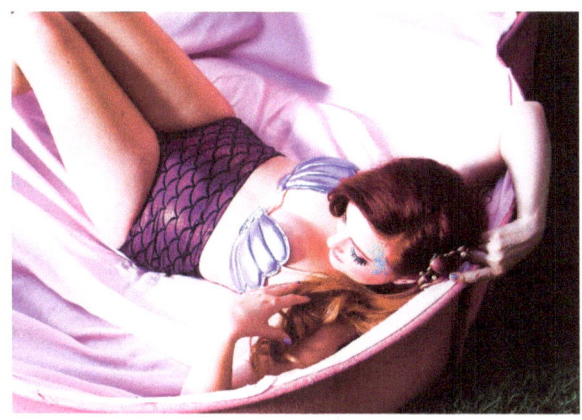

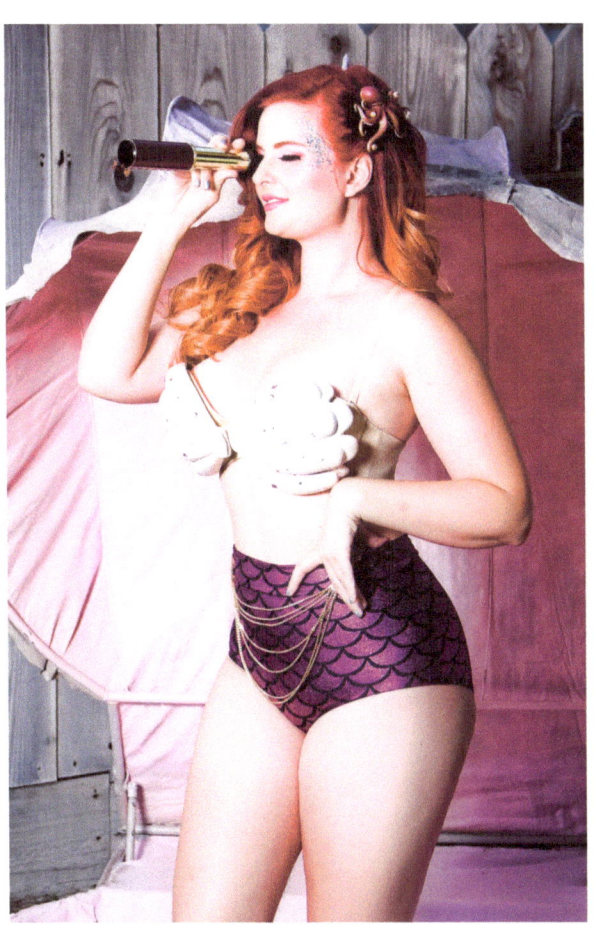

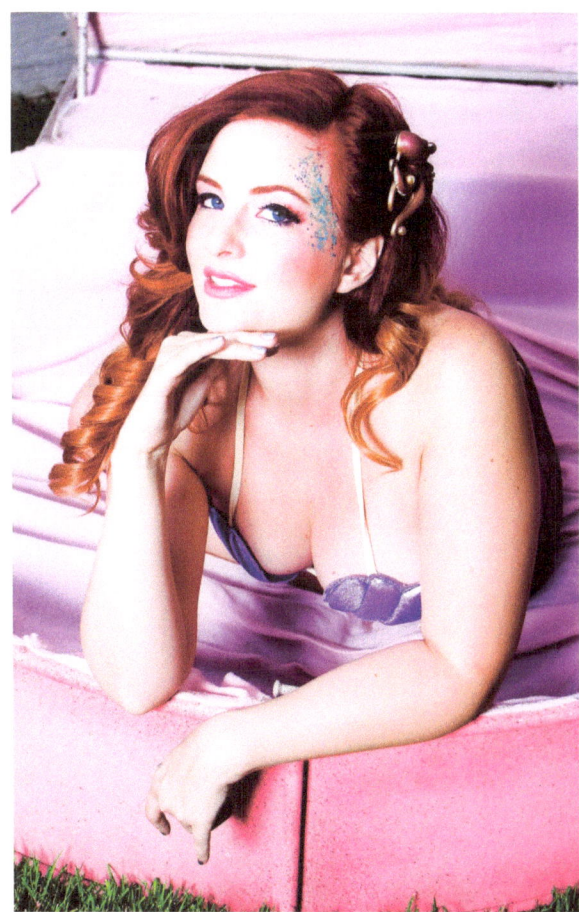

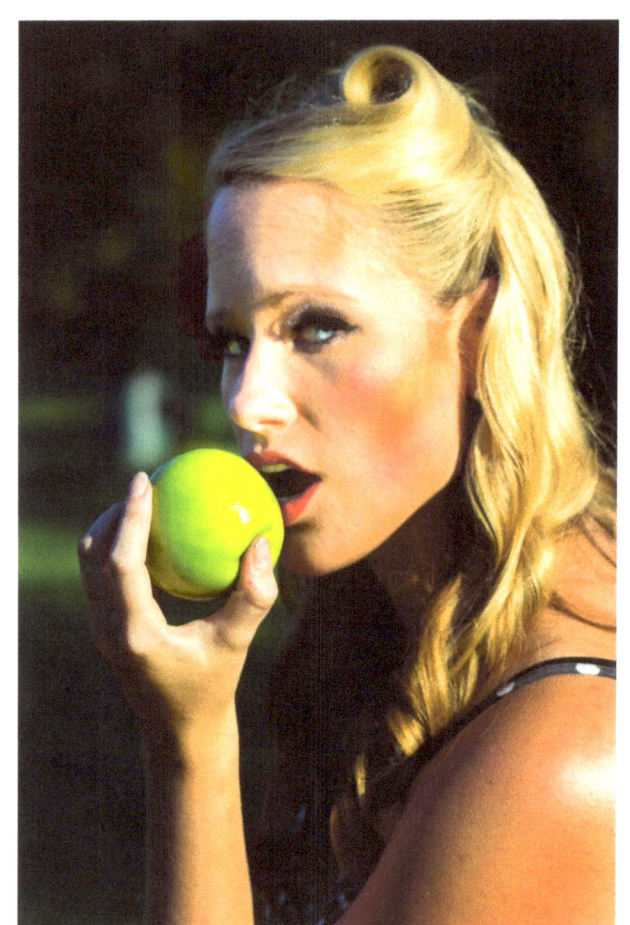
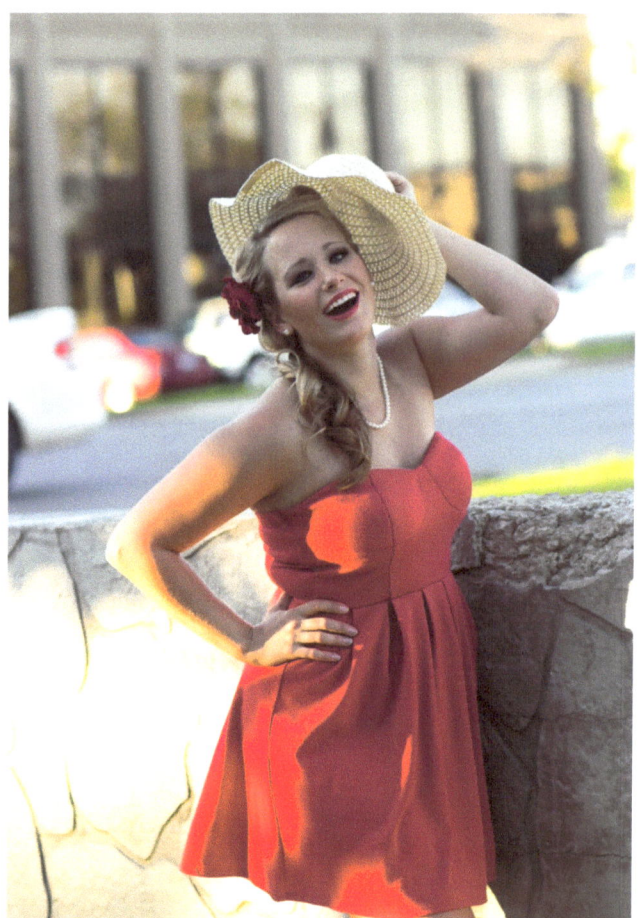

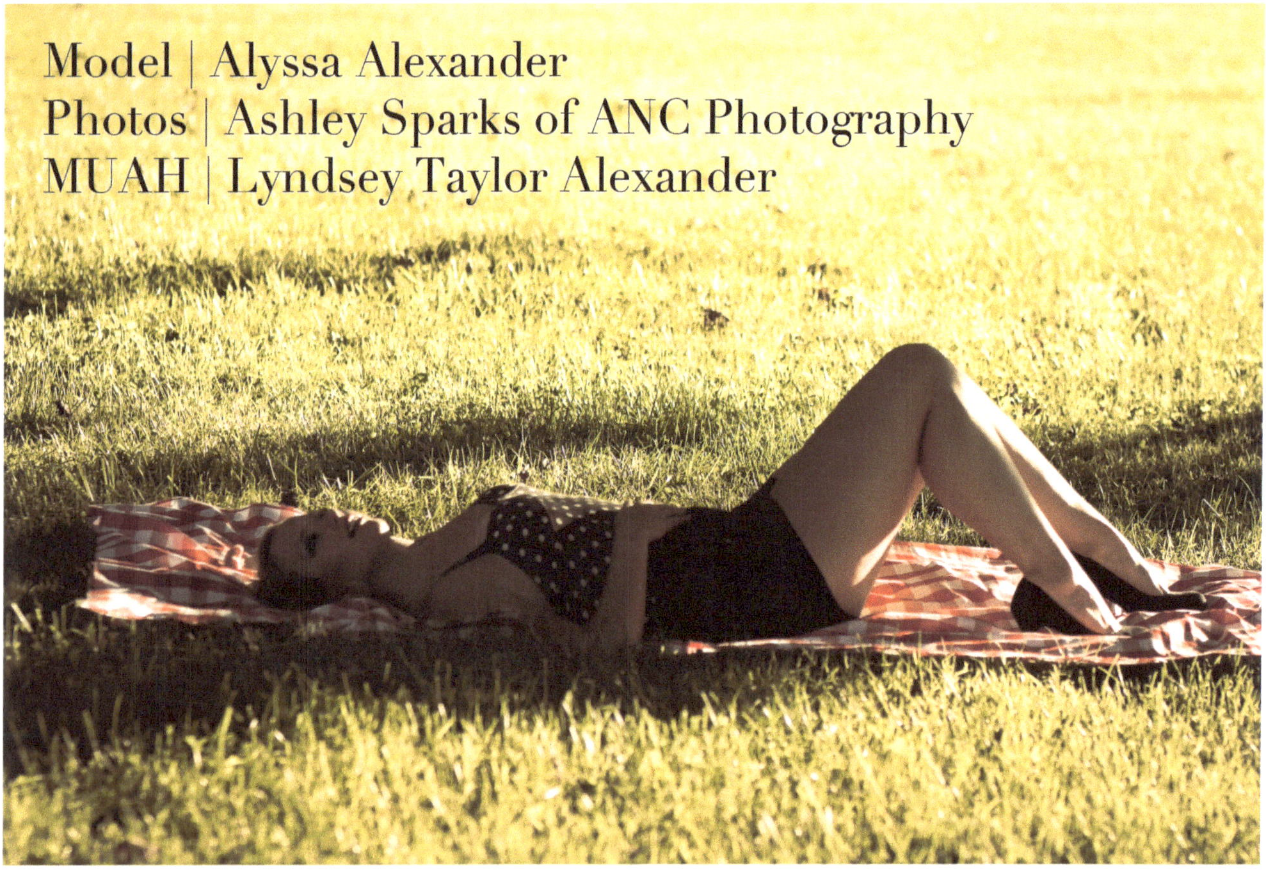

Model | Alyssa Alexander
Photos | Ashley Sparks of ANC Photography
MUAH | Lyndsey Taylor Alexander

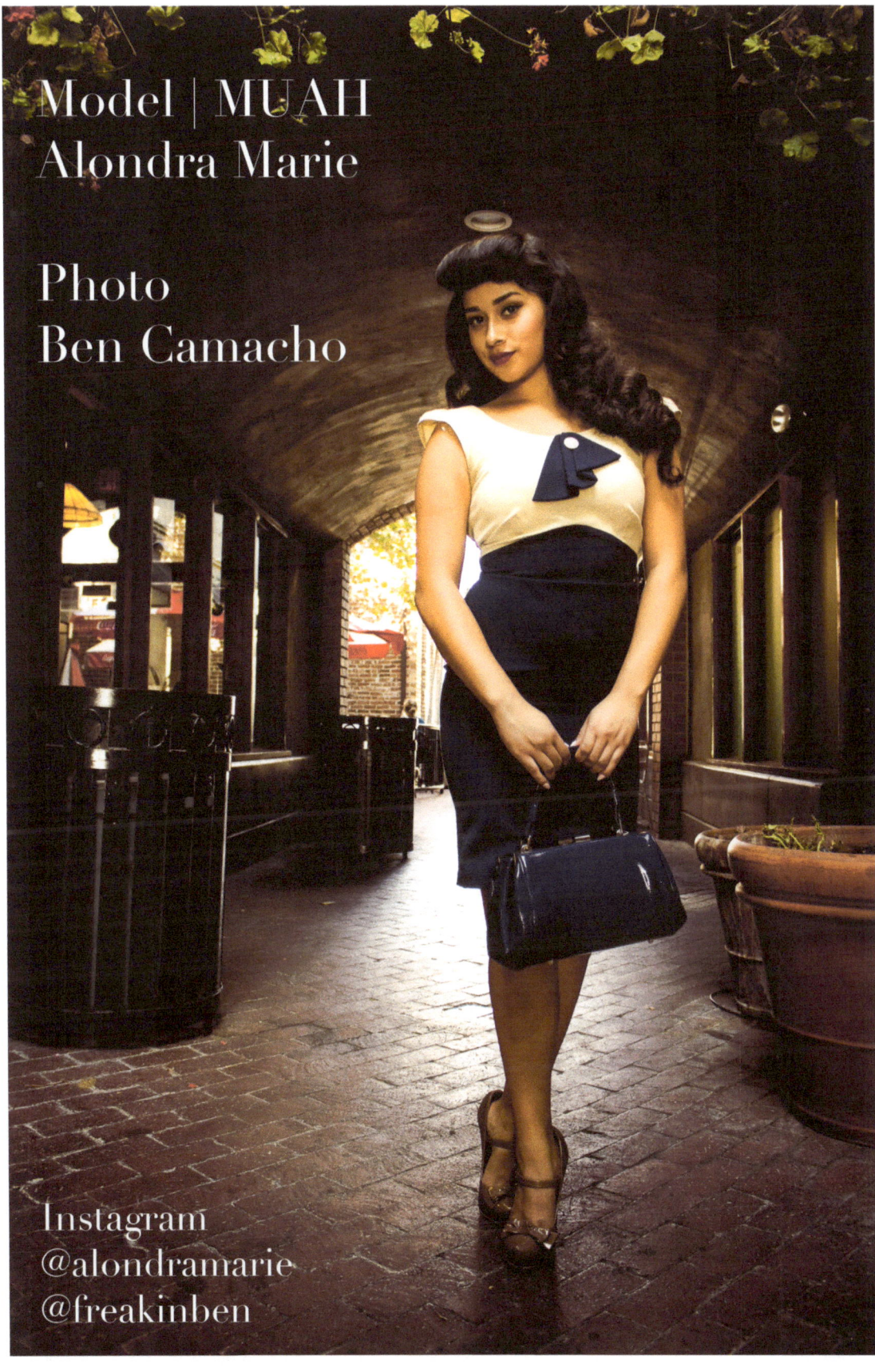

Model | MUAH
Alondra Marie

Photo
Ben Camacho

Instagram
@alondramarie
@freakinben

BRIAR ROSE

Briar Rose is a South Australian bombshell surely making a name for herself. Like a chameleon changes colour, Briar can rock a sexually charged alternative modelling gig, or strut her stuff on stage performing burlesque with grace and glamour.

In 2014 she appeared in the Wanderers Car Club annual pinup calender, rocked the stage interstate, won the title of Miss PTAA Pinup 2014, came 1st runner up in Miss Inkaholic tattoo competition, and performed alongside Adelaide's best showgirls in the 2014 Fringe Festival, and you can catch her doing it all again in 2015.

This little lady is going places and I'm sure you wouldn't want to miss a moment of it! Be sure keep an eye out for Adelaide's tattooed bombshell, Briar Rose.

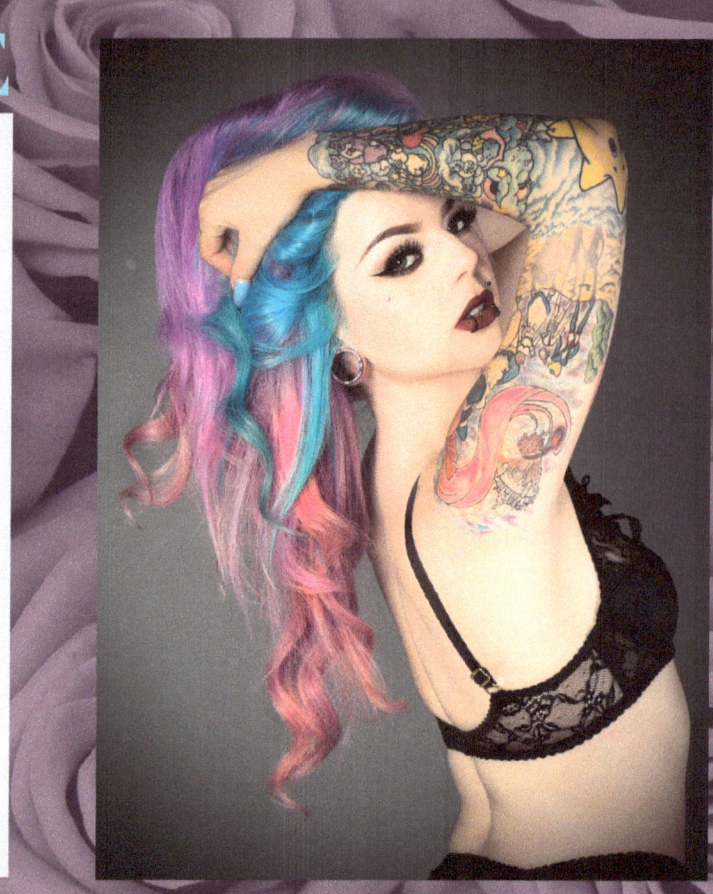

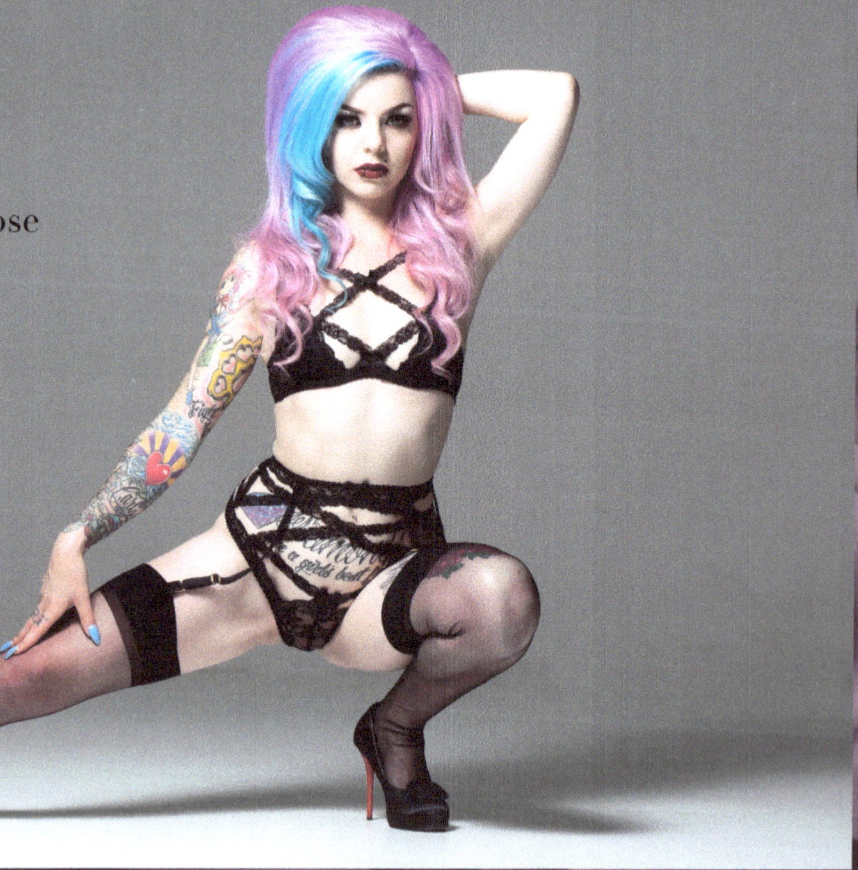

Photos by Sarah Cheesmur
Instgram @hungry4vintage

Model | MUAH | Briar Rose
facebook.com/burly.briar.rose
Instagram @asherleh

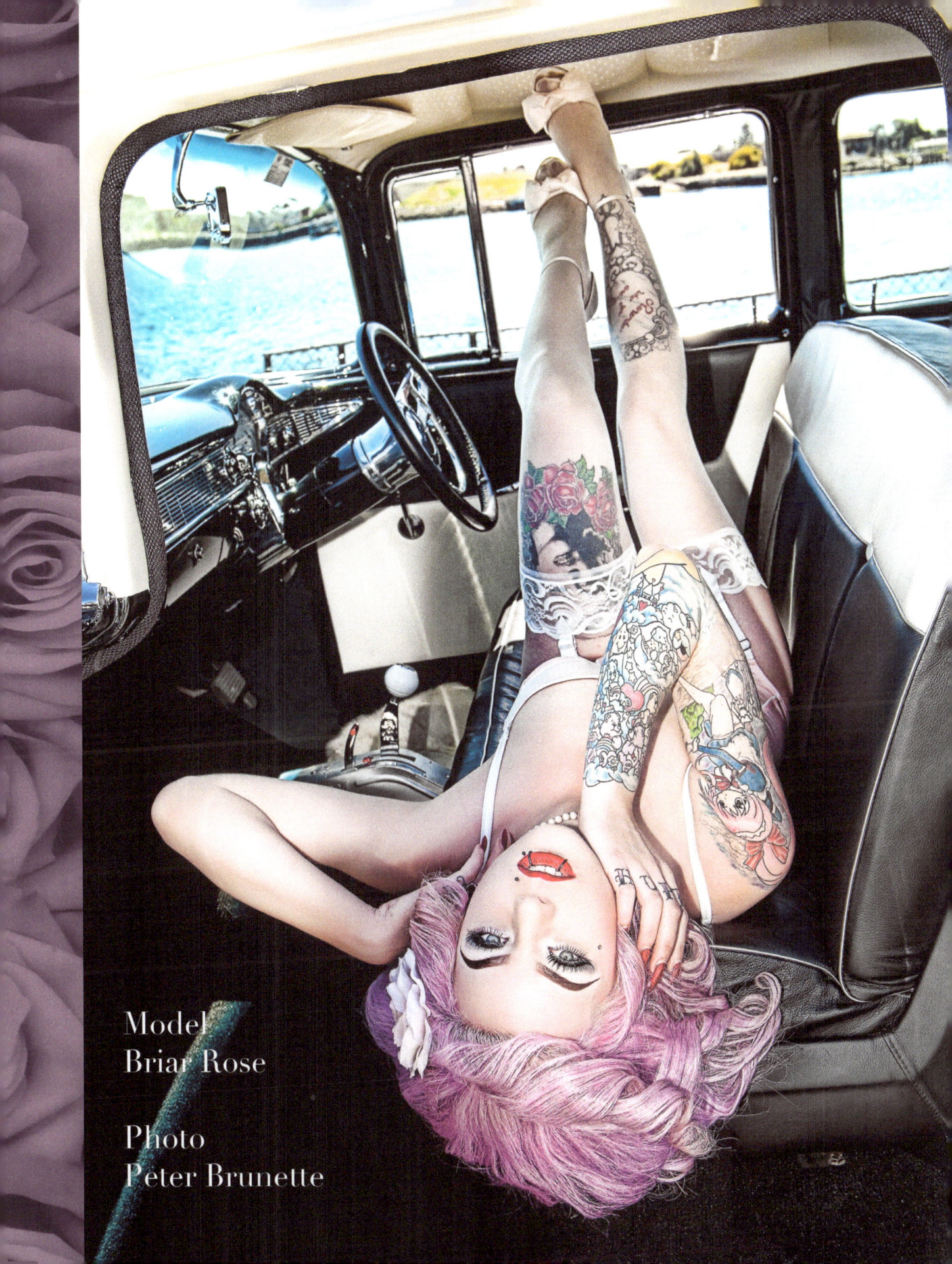

Model
Briar Rose

Photo
Peter Brunette

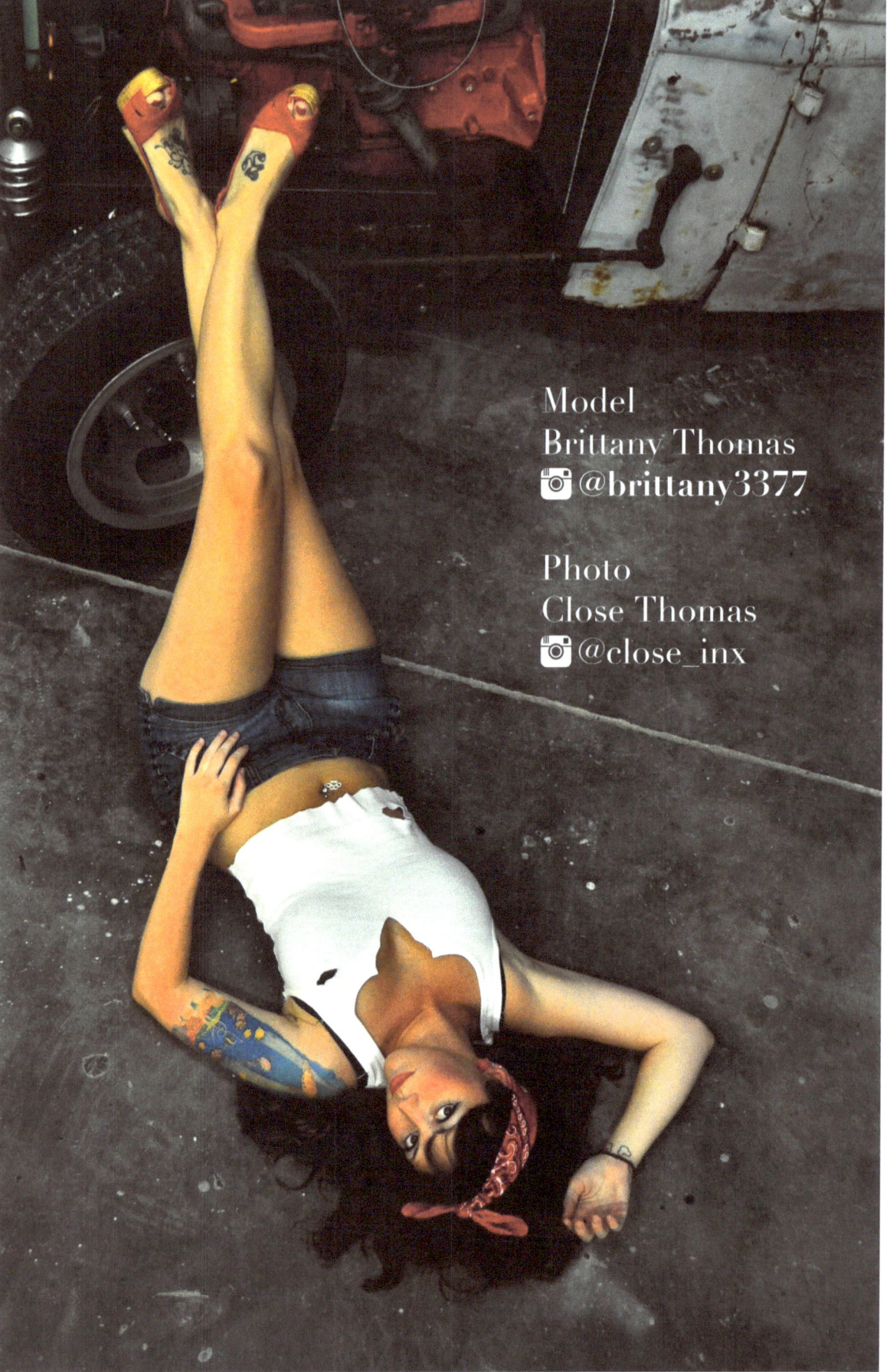

Model
Brittany Thomas
@brittany3377

Photo
Close Thomas
@close_inx

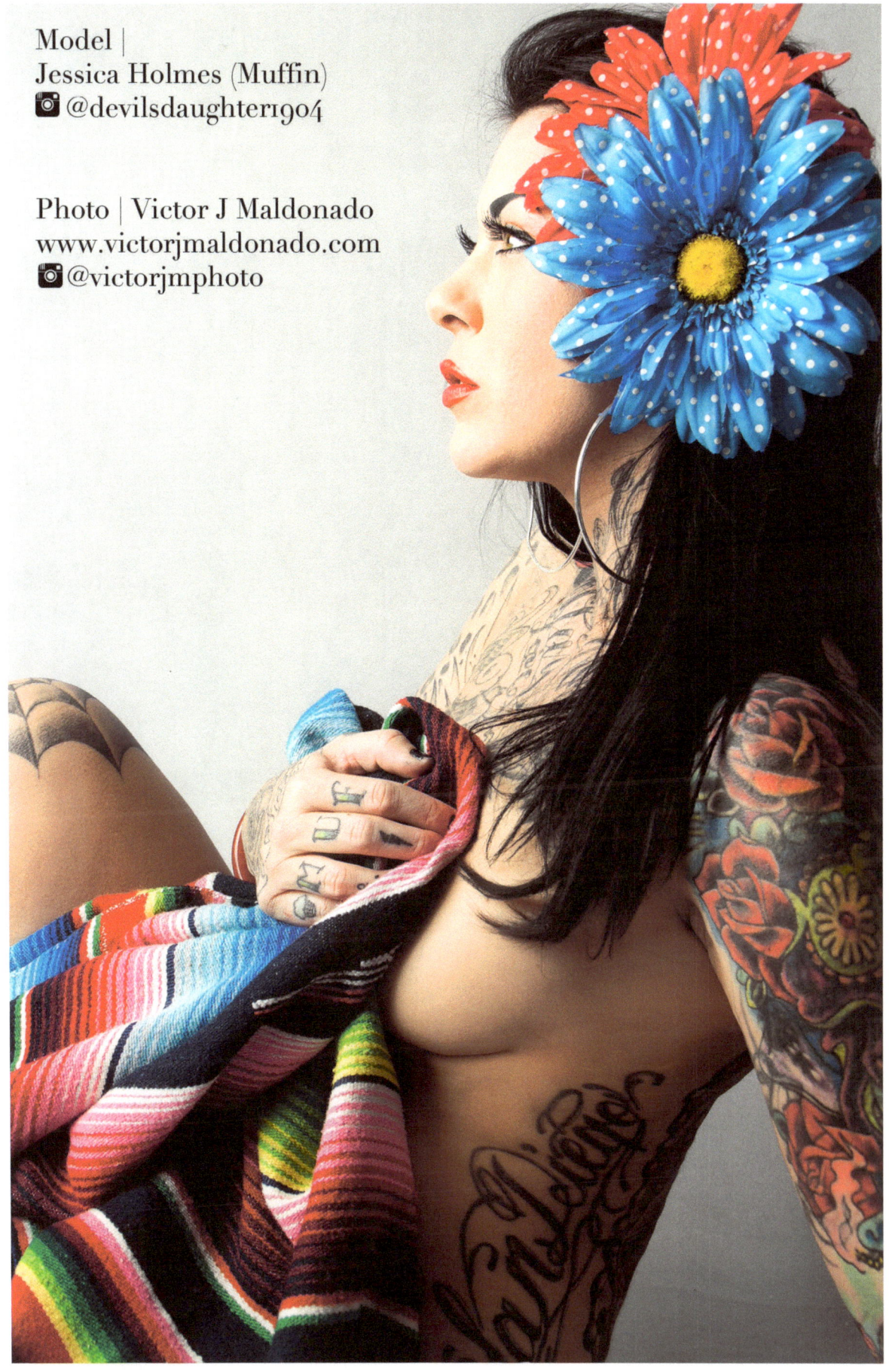

Model |
Jessica Holmes (Muffin)
@devilsdaughter1904

Photo | Victor J Maldonado
www.victorjmaldonado.com
@victorjmphoto

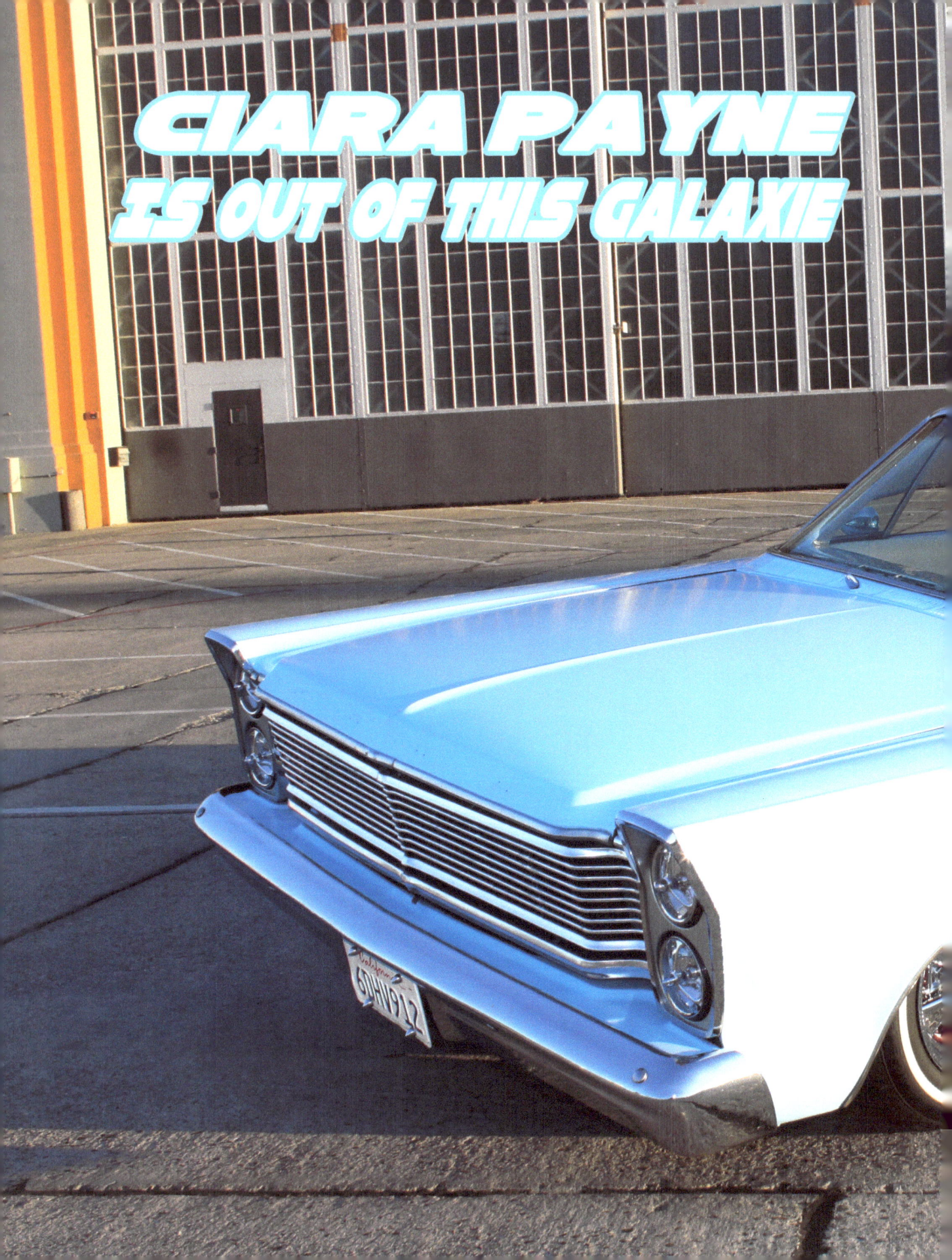

CIARA PAYNE
IS OUT OF THIS GALAXIE

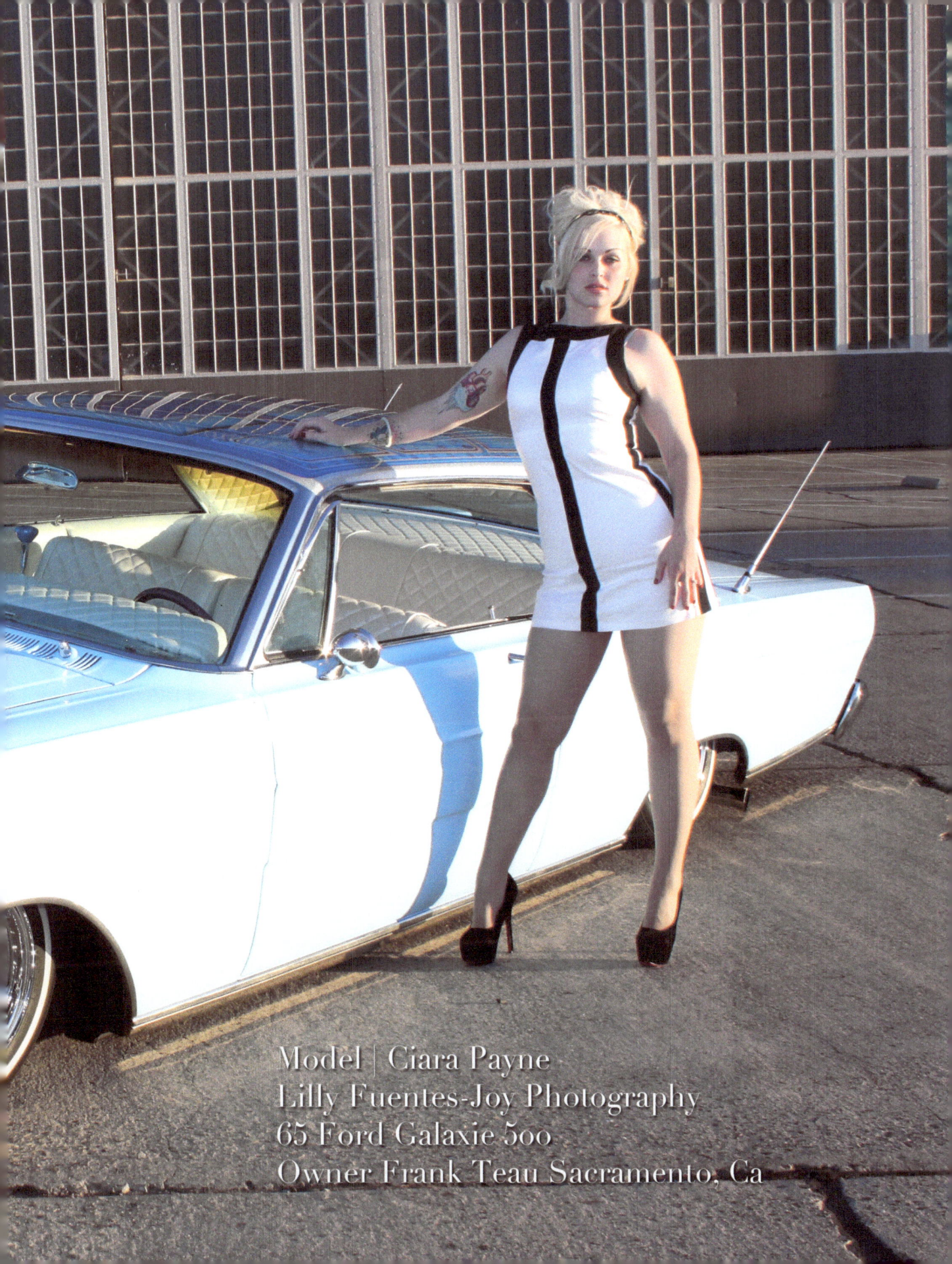

Model | Ciara Payne
Lilly Fuentes-Joy Photography
65 Ford Galaxie 5oo
Owner Frank Teau Sacramento, Ca

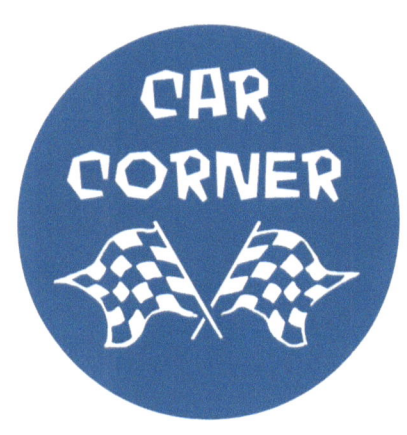

CAR CORNER

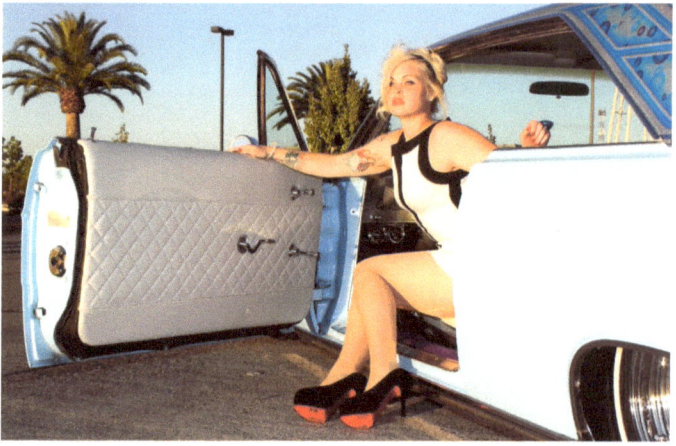

The Ford Galaxie was a full-size car built in the United States by the Ford Motor Company for model years 1959 through 1974. The name was used for the top models in Ford's full-size range from 1959 until 1961, in a marketing attempt to appeal to the excitement surrounding the Space Race. In 1962

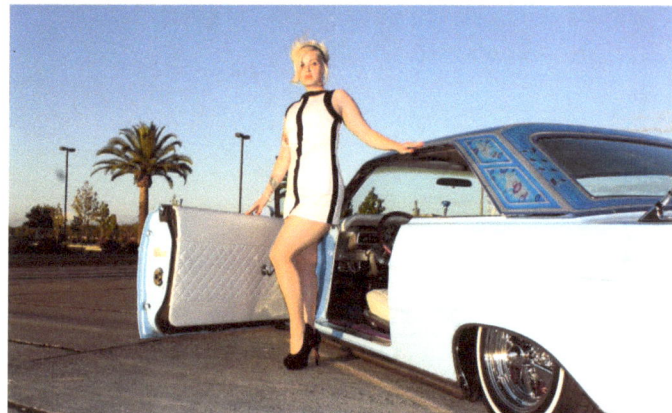

The 1965 Galaxie as seen here with the gorgeous Ciara, was an all-new design, featuring vertically stacked dual headlights in what was becoming the fashionable style in a car somewhat taller and bulkier than the previous year's. The new top-of-the-line designation this year was the Galaxie 500 LTD. Engine choices were the same as 1964, except for an all-new 240 cu in (3.9 L) six-cylinder and 1965 289 cu in (4.7 L) engine replacing the 50s-era 223 "Mileage-Maker" six and the 352 being equipped with dual exhausts and a four-barrel carburetor.

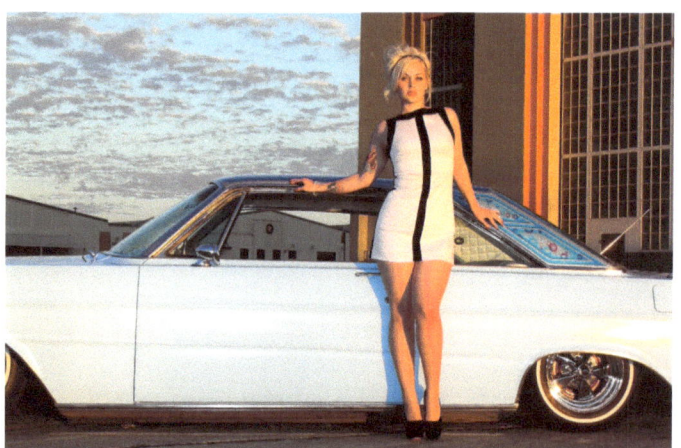

Suspension on the 1965 models was dramatically redesigned. Replacing the former leaf-spring rear suspension was a new three-link system, featuring all coils. Not only did the ride improve, but handling also got a boost, and this system was used for NASCAR in the full-size class. Interiors were like the 1964 models, but a new instrument panel and two-way key system were introduced.

Source (wikipedia.org)

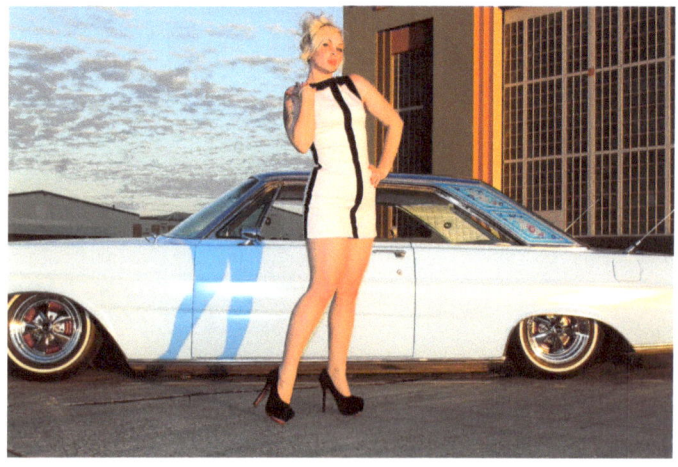

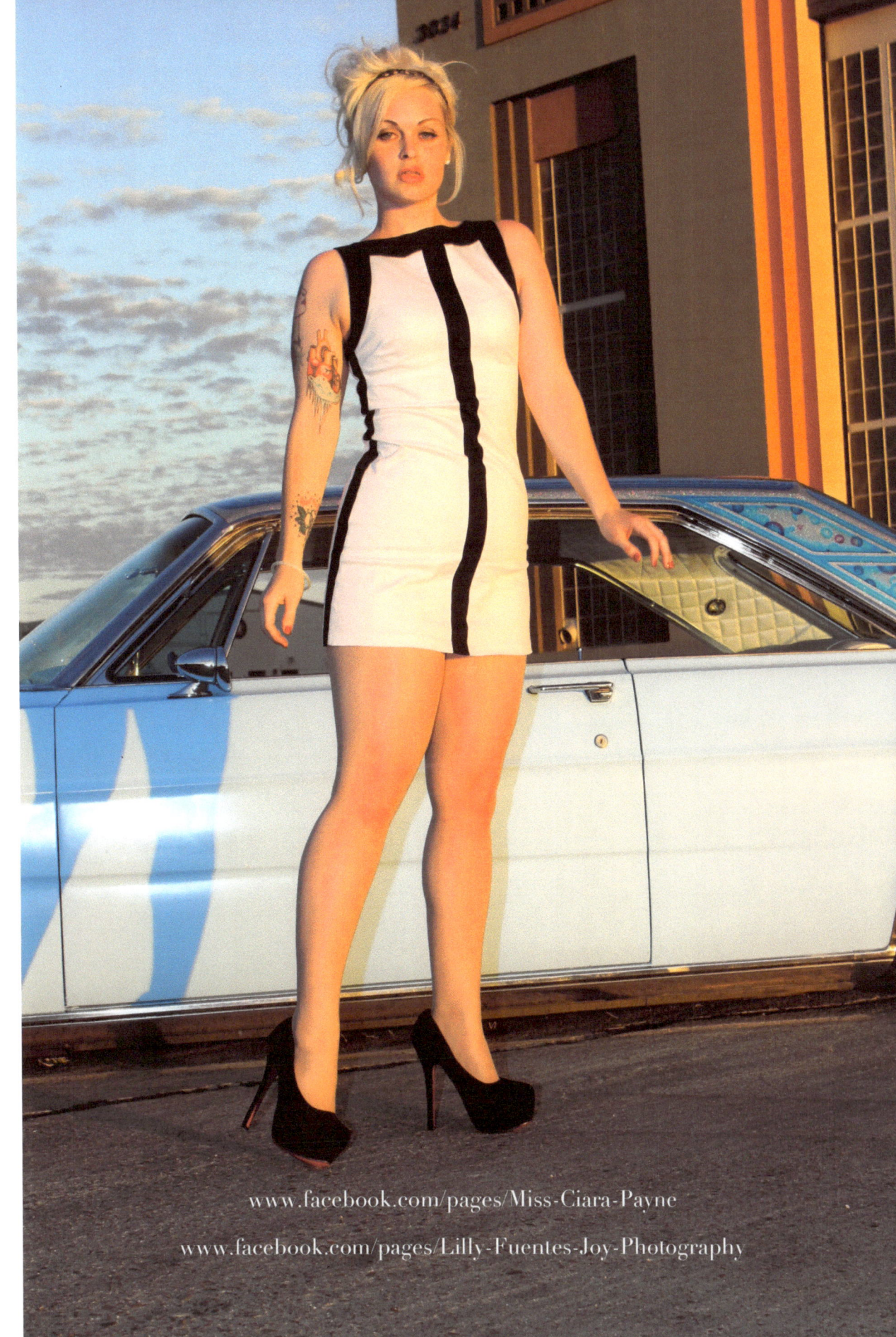

www.facebook.com/pages/Miss-Ciara-Payne

www.facebook.com/pages/Lilly-Fuentes-Joy-Photography

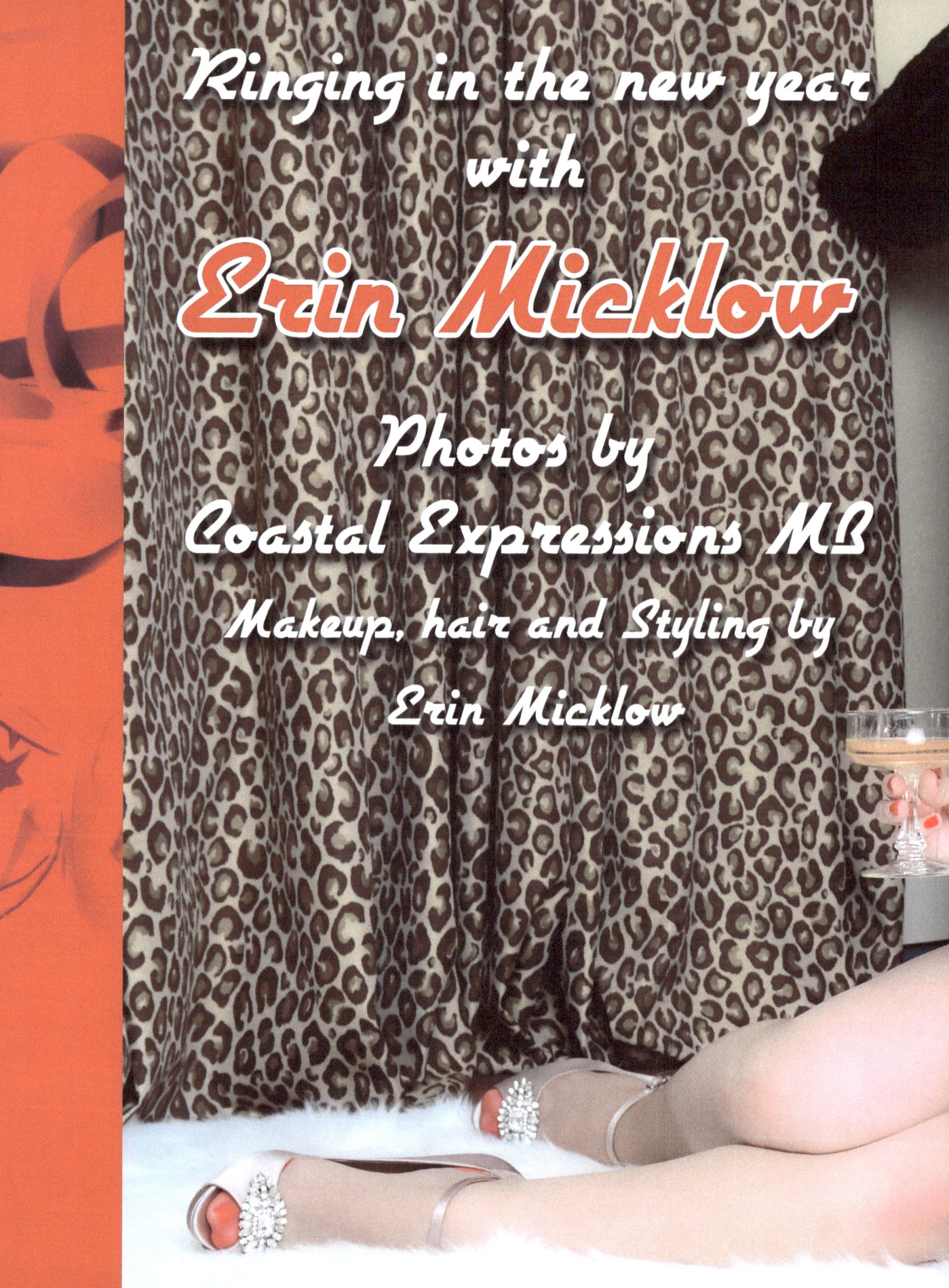

Ringing in the new year
with
Erin Micklow

Photos by
Coastal Expressions MB

Makeup, hair and Styling by

Erin Micklow

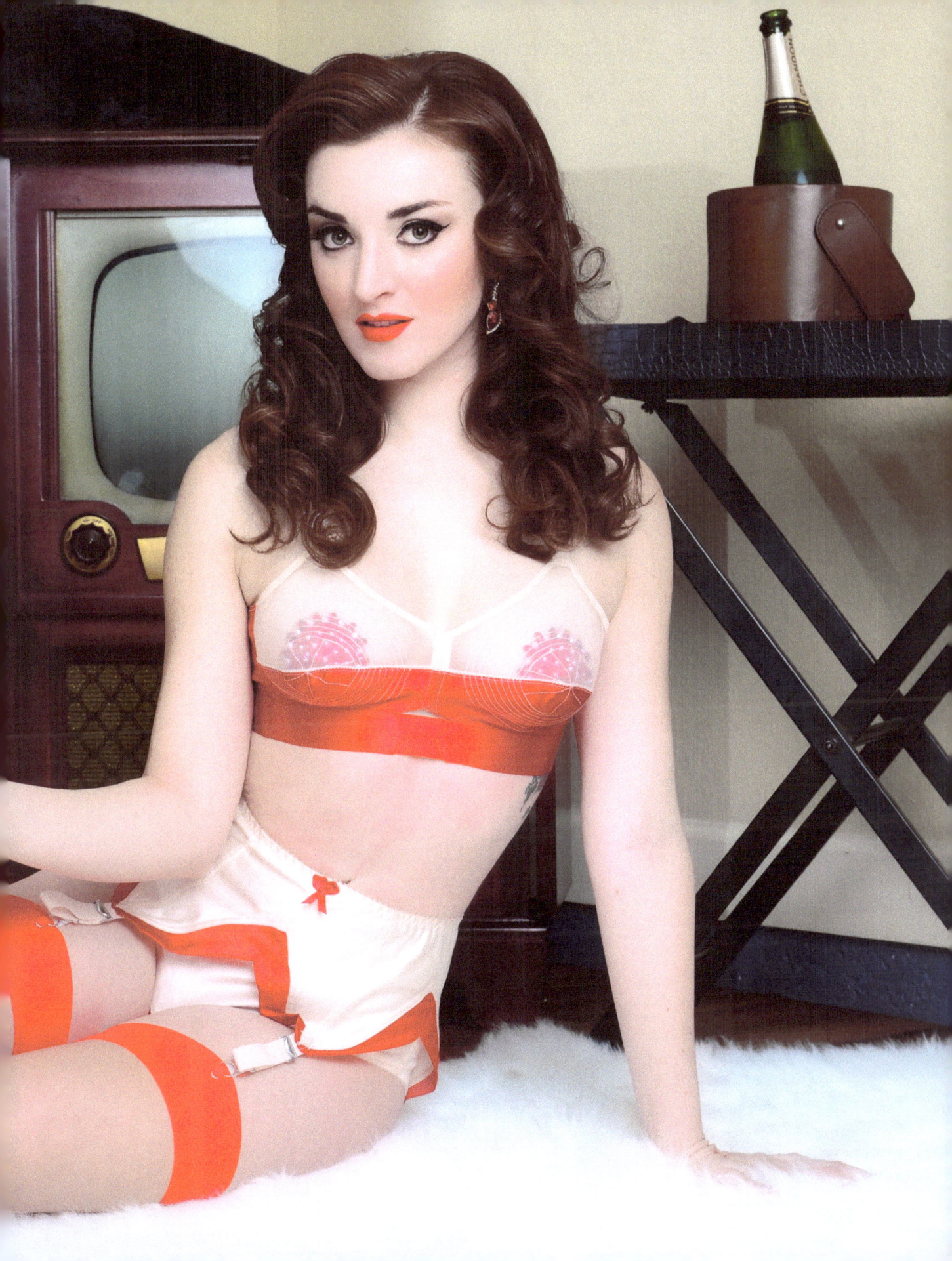

Erin Micklow, The Style Chameleon

Since 2007, Erin Micklow has been consistently working in the entertainment industry in Los Angeles as a professional model, SAG-AFTRA actress, host and dancer where she styled herself, her hair and makeup on 95% of the projects she worked on. She is known for being able to depict a wide range of looks very well. With her curvy yet athletic build, measuring 5'7" 36" (34D natural)-25"-36", Erin specializes in pinup, punk & bikini/lingerie modeling. She also has a strong social media following that loves & supports the images she makes & puts out there as well as the brands she promotes.

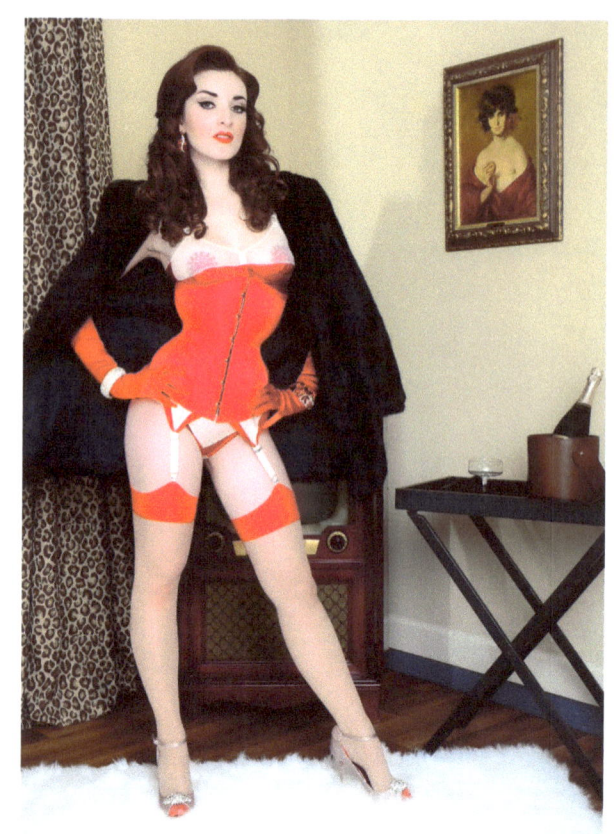

Throughout her years of being in front of the camera, Erin has graced several magazine covers and has had dozens of magazine features from publications in the US and around the world. She has also achieved commercial success modeling for companies such as got2b hair products, Hot Topic, Steady Clothing, Unique Vintage, Lucky 13 Apparel, and many more. Some of Erin's TV & film credits include Millionaire Matchmaker, The Ugly Truth, MADtv, & CSI: NY & numerous other credits on her IMDb page

In 2013, Erin branched out on her own as an independent Stylist and Image Consultant putting looks together for clients for TV, film, music videos, editorial photo shoots, as well as red carpet events. Her styling work has been featured on TMZ, Entertainment Tonight, UsWeekly, Yahoo!, AOL, Huffington Post & many more. Among her services outside of entertainment jobs, Erin offers personal shopping trips, online styling, closet raids, & travel packing. With all of that, Erin has also authored numerous fashion columns giving tips & advice to thousands of readers for publications such as Naluda Magazine, Radiant Inc Magazine, Dirtyand Thirty.com, CafeYak.com, TheStyleGlossy.com & her own personal fashion blog on ErinMicklowStylist.com.

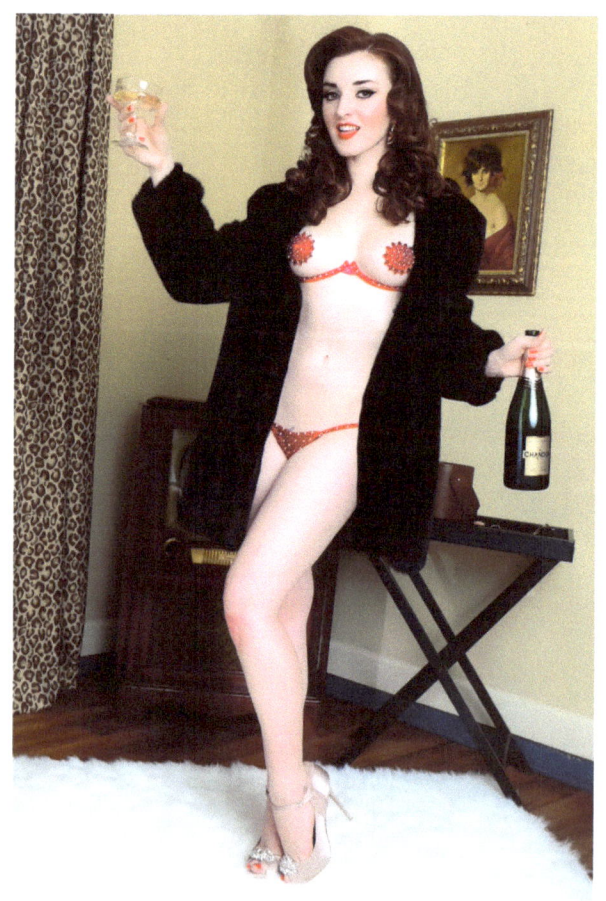

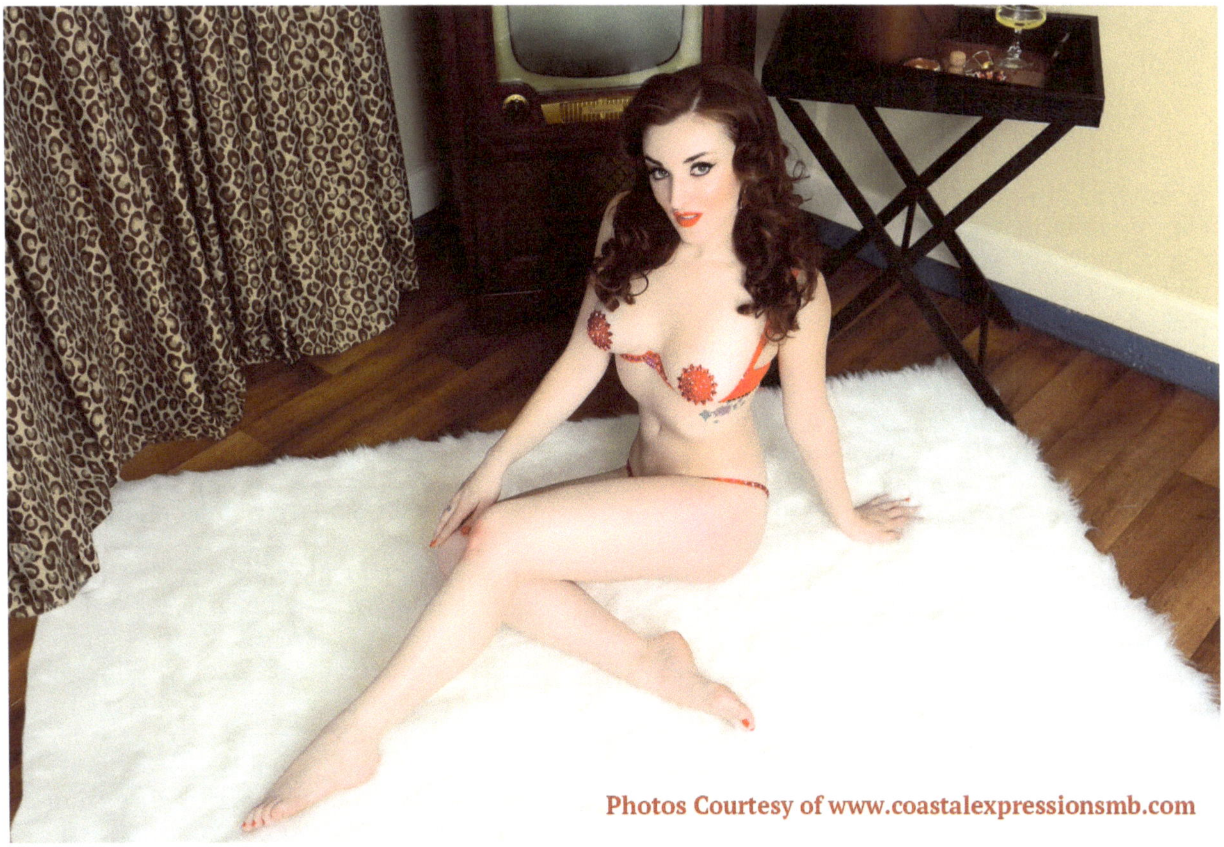

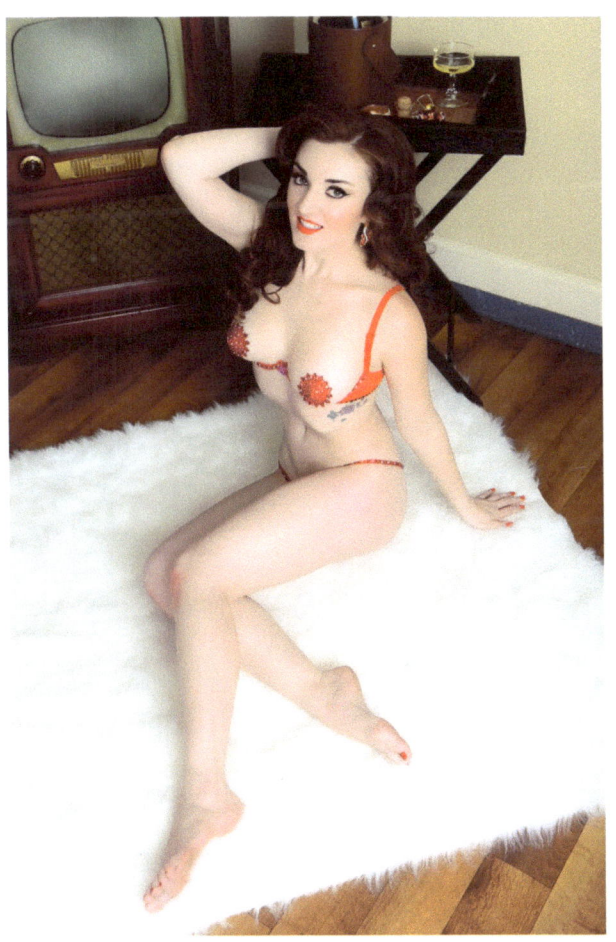

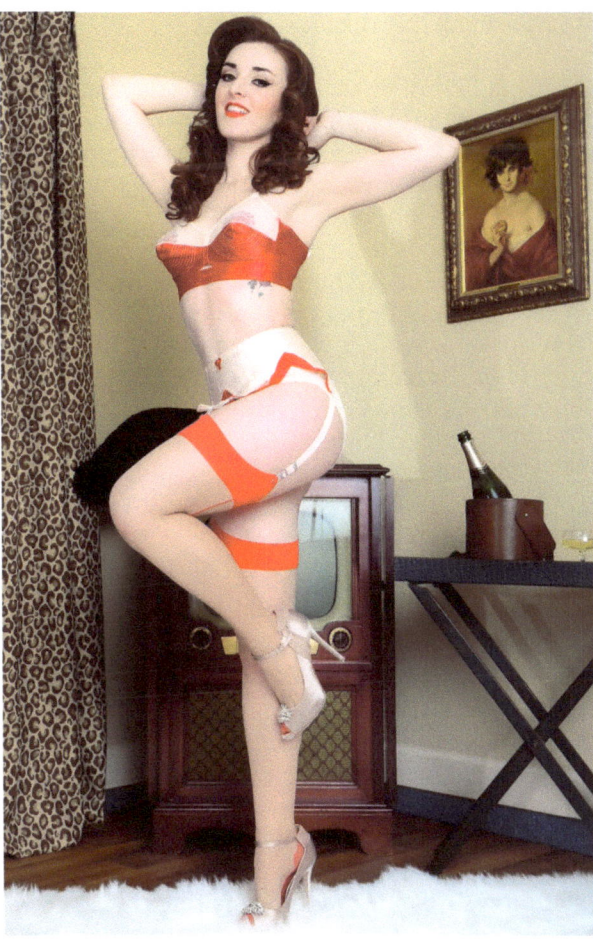

"PUNKER TURNED PINUP"

An interview with Fashion Chameleon, Erin Micklow by Jason Kamimura

Photos by Michellexstar Photography

Jason: Looking through your impressive modeling portfolio on www.ErinMicklow.com, I saw a great variety of looks that you are able to pull off equally well; from punk rock, to classic pinup and even mainstream sports modeling. Is there a particular style that you feel most comfortable doing and why?

Erin: I enjoy pinup, latex and punk modeling the most. Out of those styles I'd say I love them equally. Whenever I do a lot of pinup or latex modeling, I miss my liberty spikes, and whenever I do a lot of punk modeling, I miss being ultra girly. I try to rotate them evenly. I think it's really cool that so many people have enjoyed my punk photos. On my first photo shoot dressed like that I didn't think most people would understand it and I actually shied away from modeling like that because I didn't think anyone would like it. I think it kicks a lot of ass that I've gotten so much work having wild hair like that because it's not as common for women to have punk hair (like it is for guys).

JK: Your love of punk rock and punk fashion is evident in many of your photos. You can even be seen in a music video with *The Interrupters* featuring the legendary *Tim Armstrong* from *Rancid*! Tell me about that!

EM: Haha, yes I've known Tim since I was 17 years old. We first met at a *Rancid* show in NYC in 2006. In 2009, we reconnected in LA when I snuck backstage at a show to give him a portfolio of the punk clothes I made for girls (I wanted to have them sold on Machete Mfg). My contact info was in the portfolio & he called me the next day to talk business. We've been friends ever since.

JK: When did your love of punk begin?

EM: Punk rock found me when I was 16. This guy named Juan that sat behind me in high school and I became friends and he was a punk rocker. I didn't know what it was at the time but he was always really sweet to me and I thought he looked cool with his studded *Unseen* jacket and mohawk. Then I saw The *Unseen* were coming to town and since it was

familiar because of my friend's jacket, I decided to go. That was my first punk rock show. I never followed trends in middle and high school so I was made fun of a lot and often called "weird". I didn't have many friends (not for lack of trying) and the "friends" I did have were pretty shitty. So for me, punk felt like a home. Something I could rely on when I was lonely. The music kept me company and the shows were a place to meet people that looked even weirder than me.

JK: In addition to modeling I noticed that you are a SAG/AFTRA actress and have several IMDB credits to your name. Is acting something that you wish to pursue? What are your goals as an actress?

EM: Yes, I am a proud union member! I currently do have an acting agent and go on auditions occasionally. At the moment, it's not something I'm actively pursuing, but when opportunities and auditions come up, I take them if my schedule allows it.

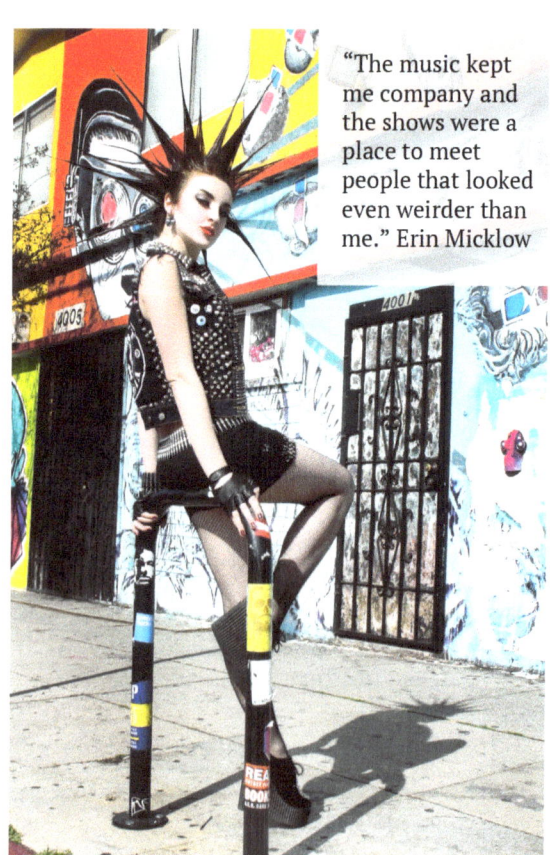

"The music kept me company and the shows were a place to meet people that looked even weirder than me." Erin Micklow

JK: One of the things that caught my eye about you in addition to your obvious beauty is that you do your own hair, makeup and styling most of the time. Is that something you taught yourself or did you take classes in cosmetology?

EM: Thank you! Those are skills I learned from working with talented hair and makeup artists (and asking them tons of questions), YouTube tutorials from various people, and persistence. It's such a valuable skill to be able to do your own hair and makeup. It's a treat to have a talented artist do my hair and makeup for me, but there's not always room in the budget or an artist available. I was motivated to learn to do myself up so that I wouldn't always have to rely on someone else to help me get ready.

JK: You have an amazingly tiny waist. I know corset training has become popular lately, is that something that you practice? If not what kind of work out regiment do you do to stay in shape?

EM: With the growing popularity and trendiness of waist training right now, this is a question I've been asked more frequently. I do waist train with a custom wasp waist corset, but one thing to keep in mind about the subject is that waist training won't necessarily make you thinner. It's more about creating a more defined waist. So in addition to waist training, I am on a fitness diet of eating low calorie meals and snacks every few hours (heaviest meals in the morning, lightest meals in the evening), limited alcohol intake and exercise. I workout 3-4 times a week and stay active in between workouts.

JK: When you are not working as a fashion stylist, model, actress and general bad ass what do you do for fun?

EM: Haha, I love to travel! I would travel all the time if I could afford it. This year I've been really lucky to travel a lot for work in addition to my regular yearly trips. Every year I always try to go somewhere I've never been for my birthday (if you have to get older you might as well do something fabulous!) so this year I visited Jamaica which was an amazing adventure. -

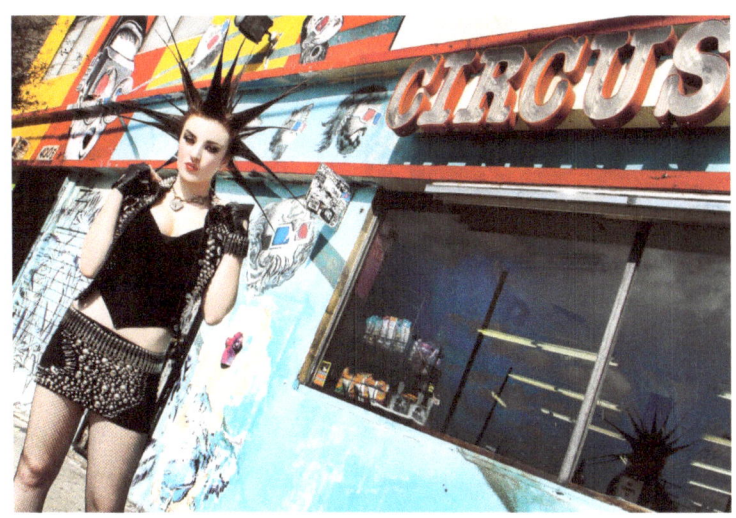

Then there's Germany which is like my second home now. My husband is German and immigrated to America when we got married 2 1/2 years ago, so we go back at least once a year so he can see his family and friends. He's from a really small country town in Bavaria where no one really speaks English, so while he visits with his family/friends, I take a 6 hour train ride up to Berlin and usually stay for a week or so. To me, Berlin is a magical city (and they have a strong punk scene). I've made so many friends from the U.S. and all other parts of the world in Berlin, and we seem to have a really tight bond. It's strange, but awesome and very special.

JK: As an experienced model what advice would you give to models who are just starting out?

EM:
1) Work hard 2) Be persistent 3) Always try to make your next shoot better than your last 4) Pay attention to detail 5) Conduct yourself in a professional manner

JK: That sounds like fantastic advice! What are some of your goals for the future?

EM: To continue what I'm doing at a steady incline!

JK: Good answer Erin!

**For more about Erin, please visit
www.ErinMicklow.com
and
www.ErinMicklowStylist.com**

**Follow Erin:
IG/Twitter: @erin_micklow**

Facebook: www.facebook.com/ErinMicklowOfficial

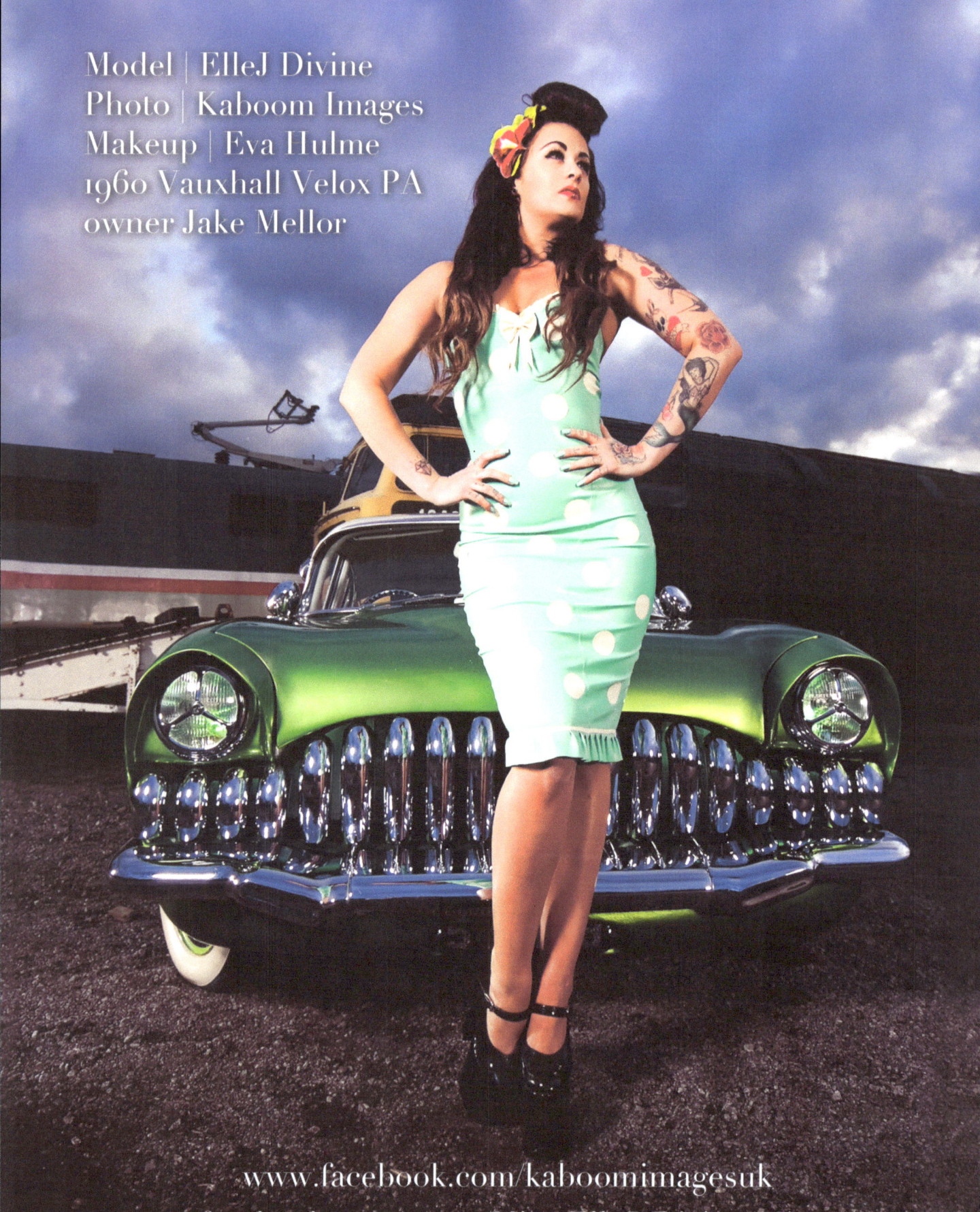

Model | ElleJ Divine
Photo | Kaboom Images
Makeup | Eva Hulme
1960 Vauxhall Velox PA
owner Jake Mellor

www.facebook.com/kaboomimagesuk
www.facebook.com/pages/Miss-ElleJ-Divine-Miss-Ljay

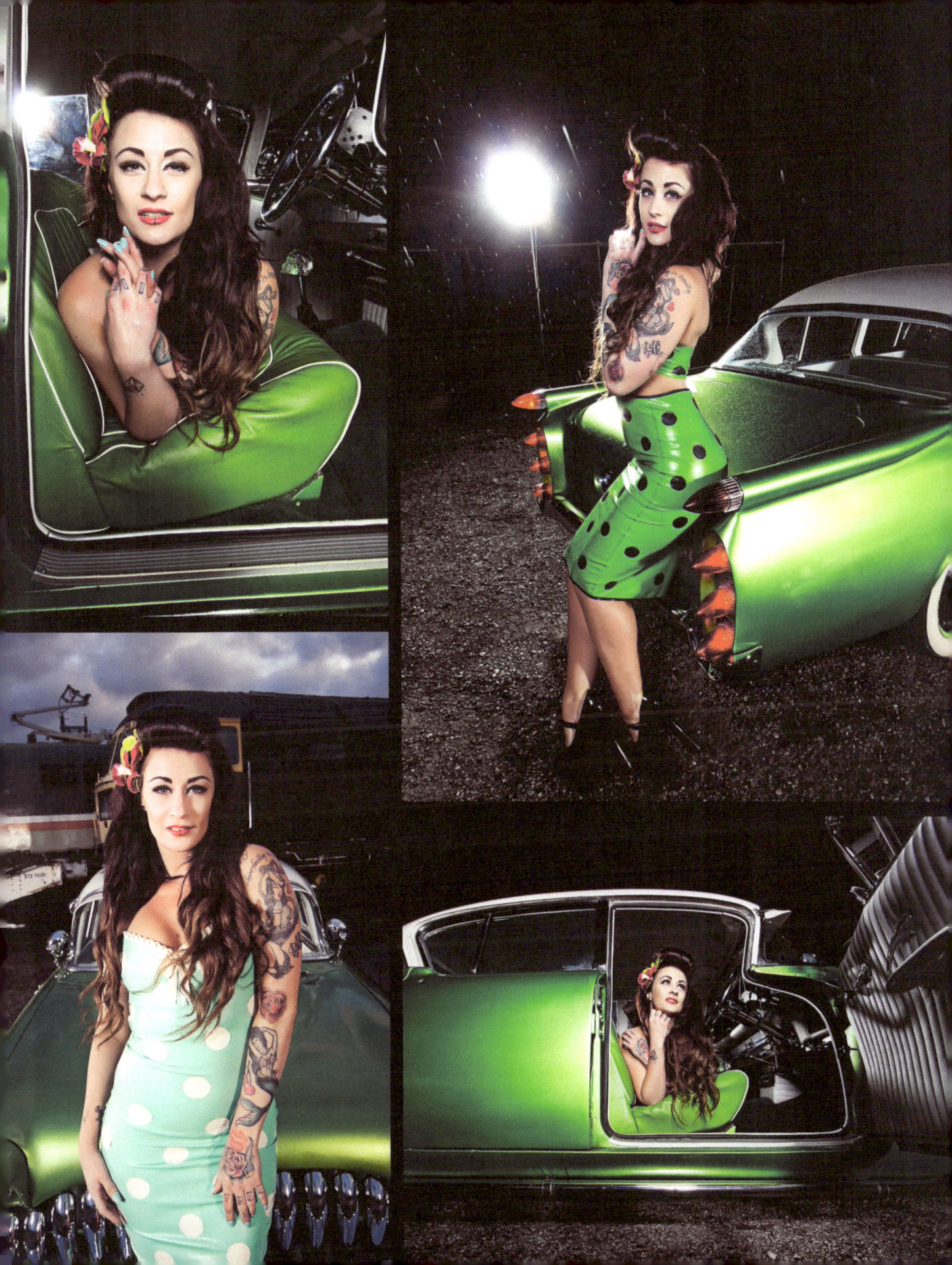

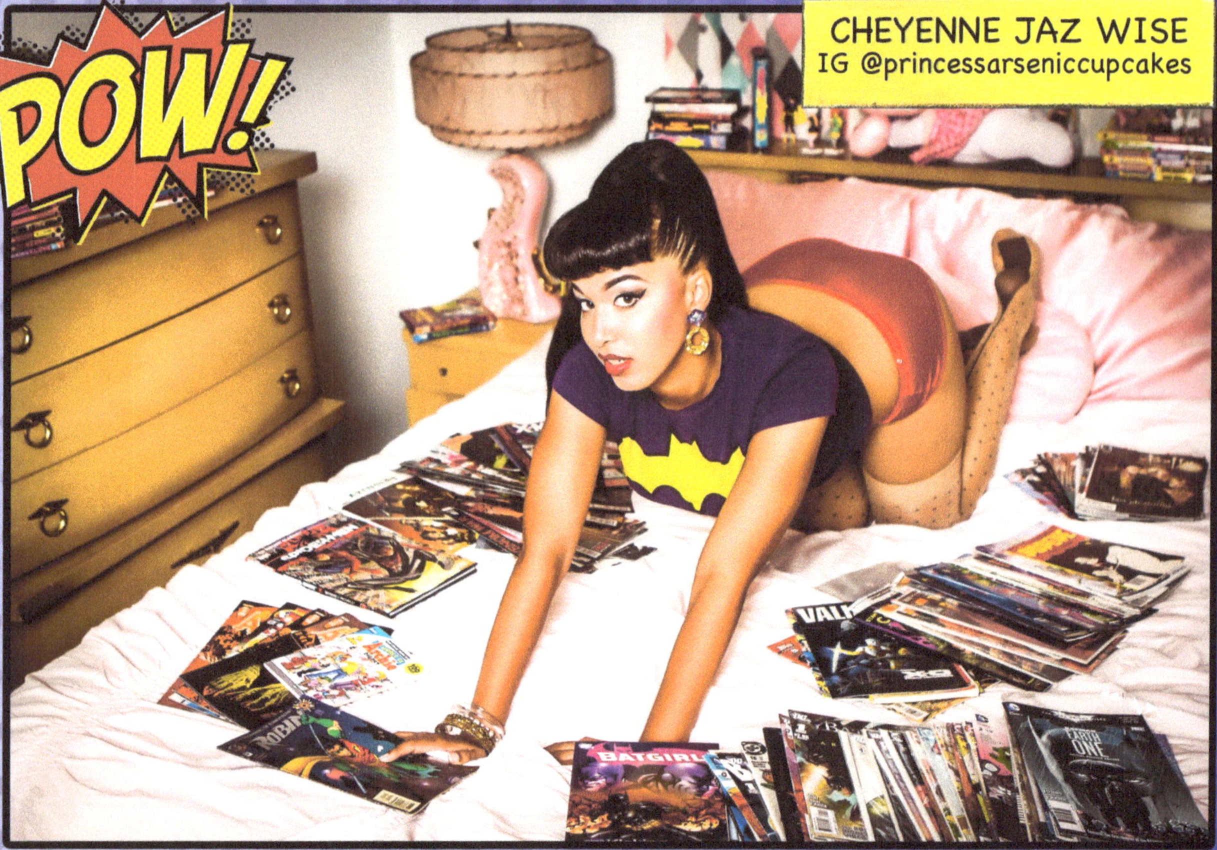

POW!

CHEYENNE JAZ WISE
IG @princessarseniccupcakes

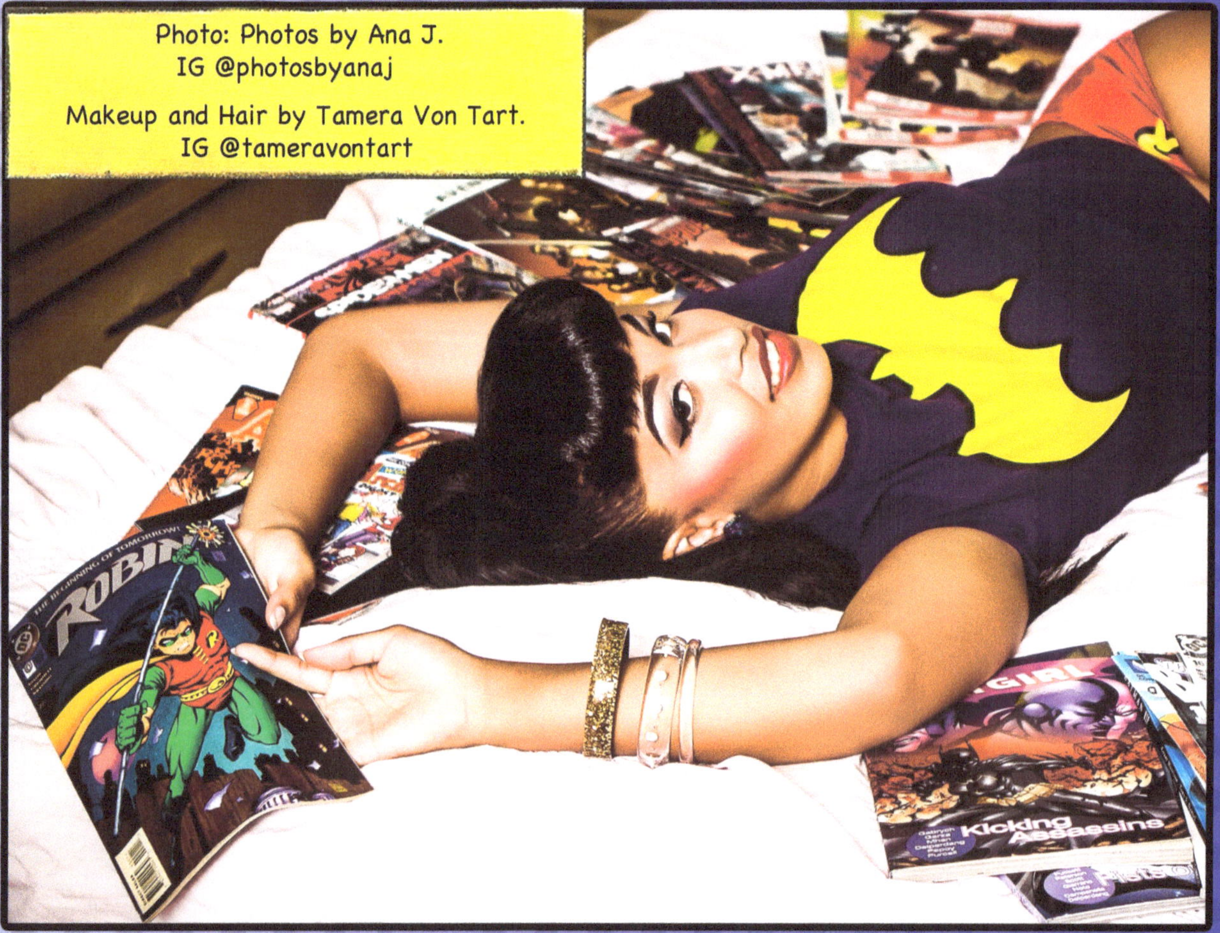

Photo: Photos by Ana J.
IG @photosbyanaj

Makeup and Hair by Tamera Von Tart.
IG @tameravontart

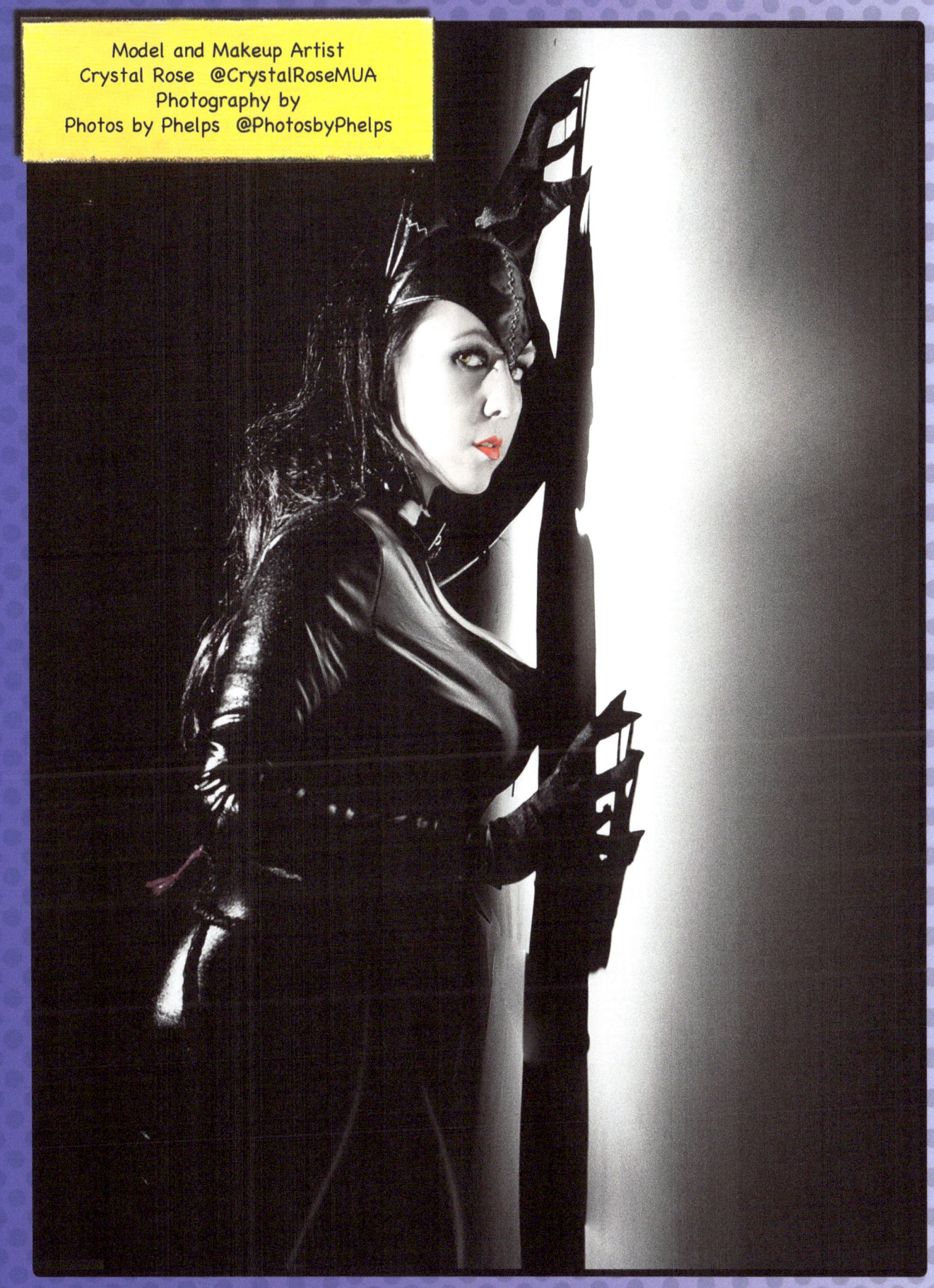

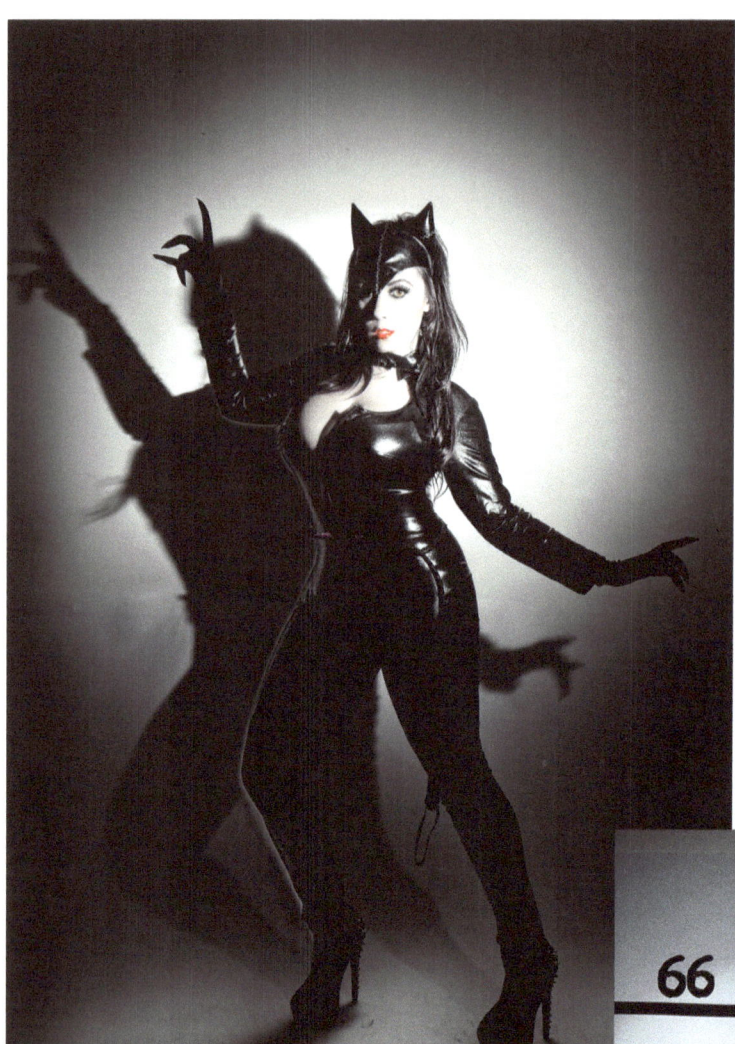

Crystal Rose is a multi-published model based in Central New Jersey. She specializes in Pin-Up, Glam, and Eye Candy styles. As you can see from this shoot, she also likes to play dress up from time to time and is a fan of **Cosplay, Batman, Who Framed Roger Rabbit and Pee Wee Herman!**

When she is not modeling, Crystal works as a Certified Makeup Artist, and did all of her own hair and makeup for these shoots with James Phelps. Her fantastic looks along with her fun sparkling personality have gained her a following of over 20 thousand followers and growing on facebook!

Follow her (In a non creepy way) at

www.facebook.com/crystalrosethemodel or on Instagram @crystalrosemua

James Phelps is a Published Baltimore Native photographer with shooting experience starting in 2007. James shoots anything from head shots, to dancer flyers, to website content, "I will photograph someone as long as they have a vision and desire. I don't limit who should be in front of my camera," says James who specializes in Glam, Edge , Eye candy and Plus size models. "I make pretty people..Prettier," says James, and from what I have seen of his work this statement is true. With over 50 thousand followers on facebook alone, he must be doing something right!

www.facebook.com/photosbyphelpsfanpage
Email: photosbyphelps@gmail.com
Instagram: photosbyphelps
www.modelmayhem.com/448473

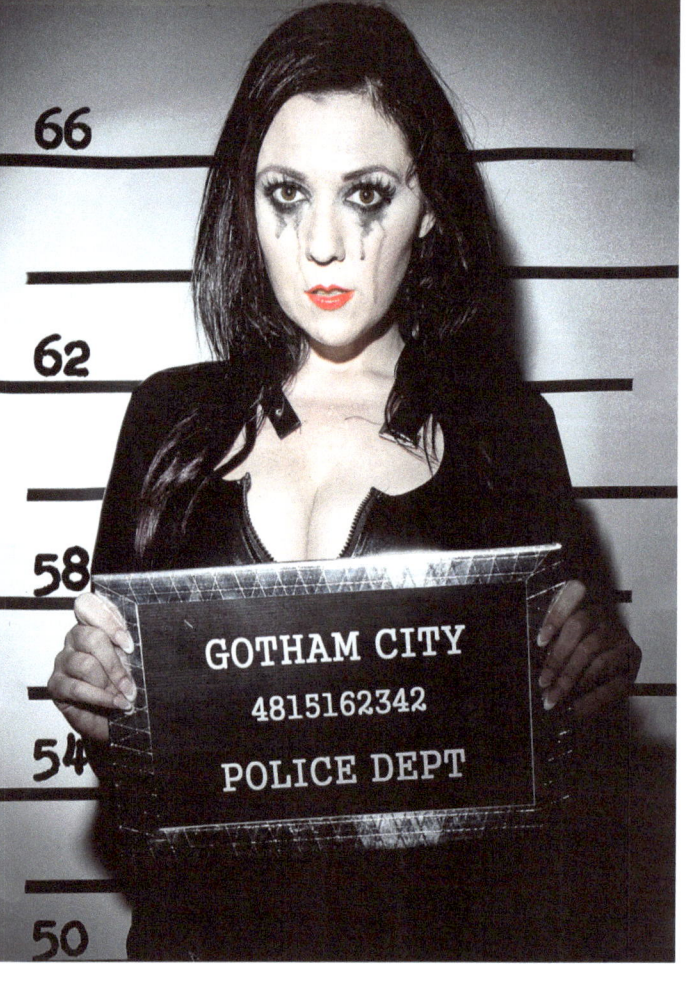

66

62

58

54

50

GOTHAM CITY

4815162342

POLICE DEPT

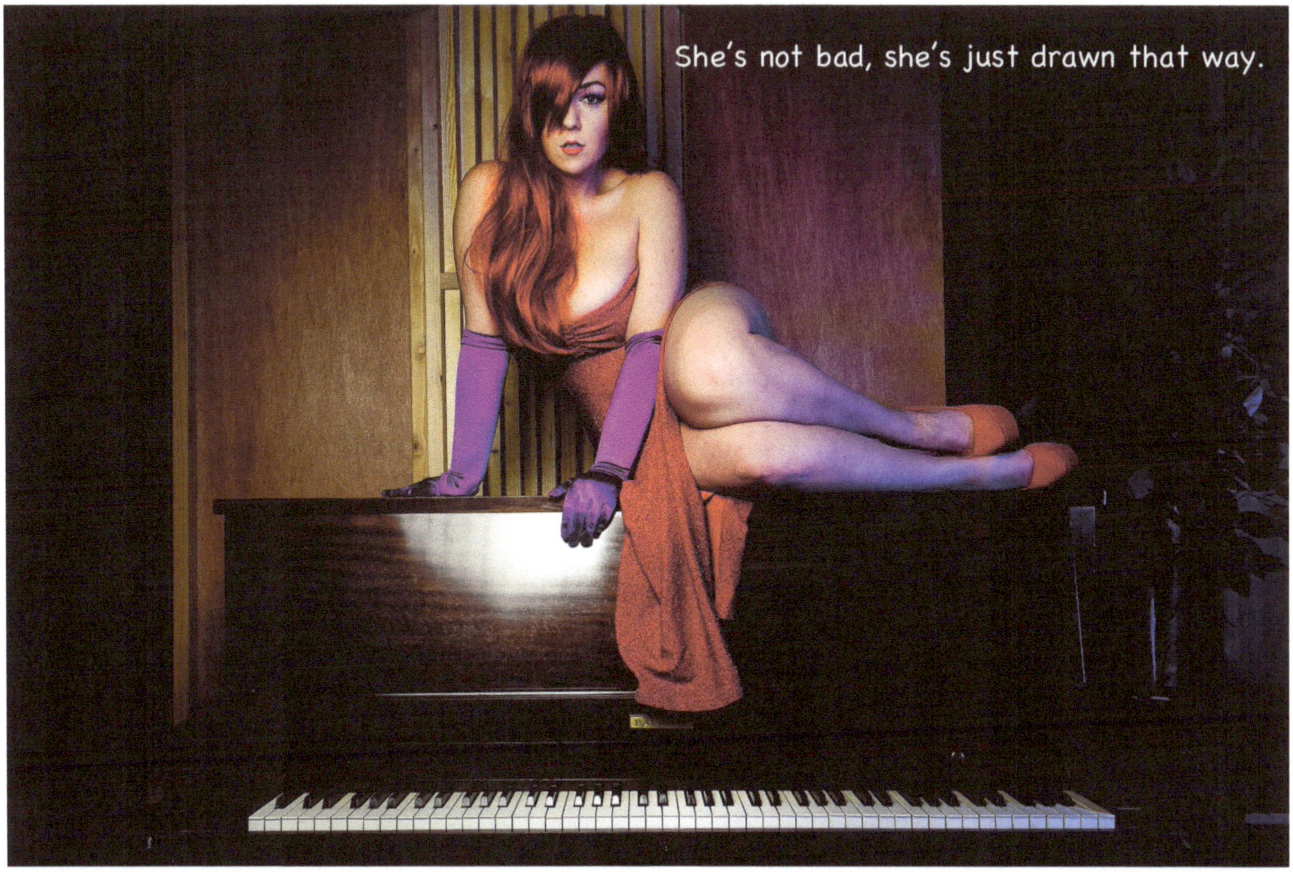

She's not bad, she's just drawn that way.

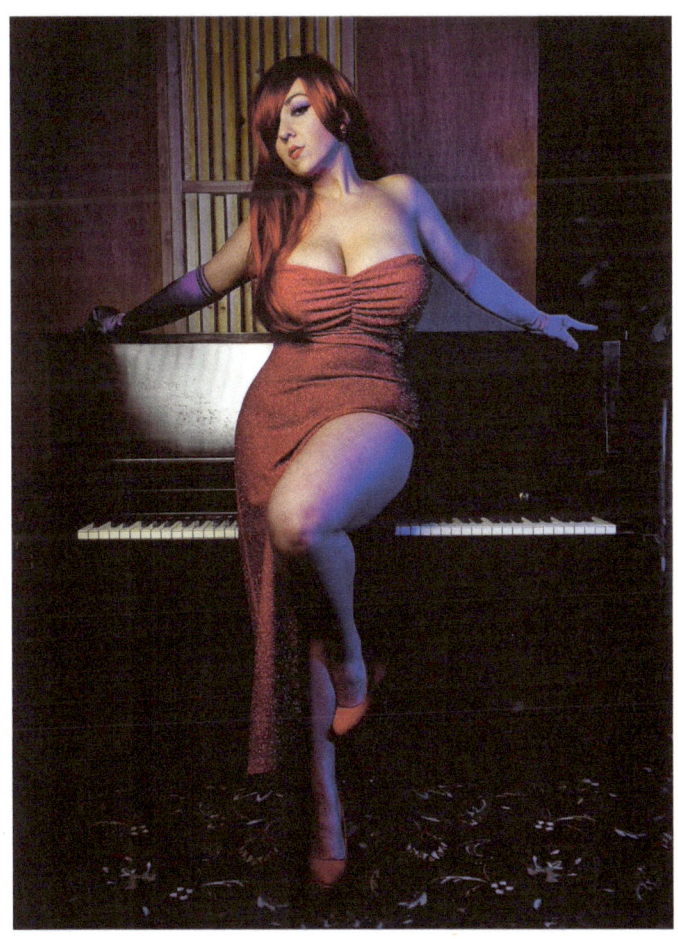
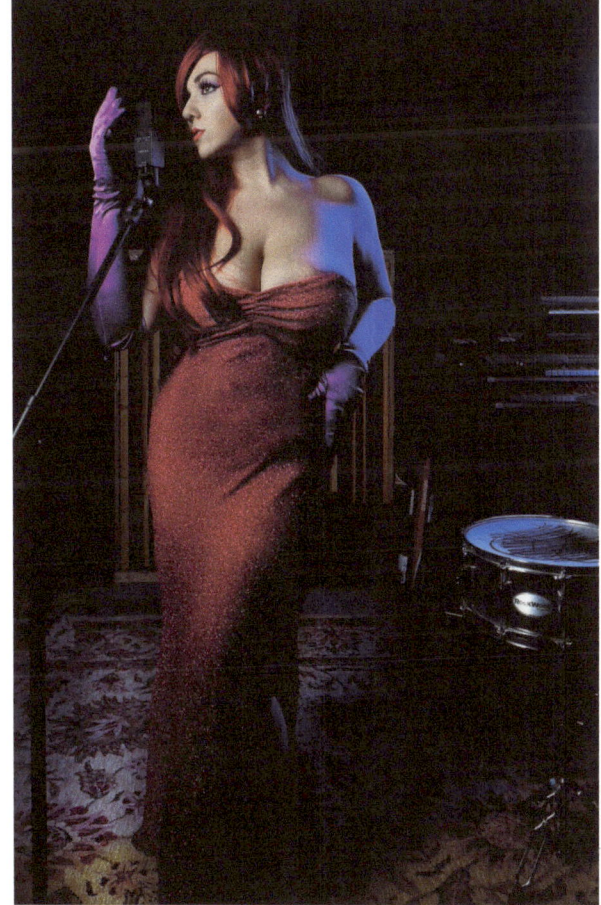

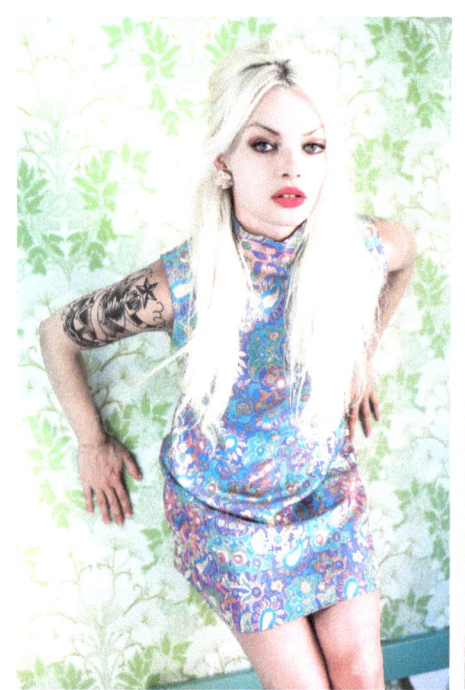 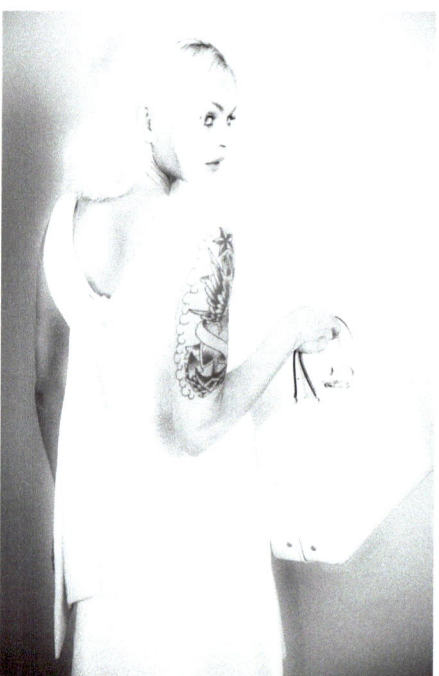 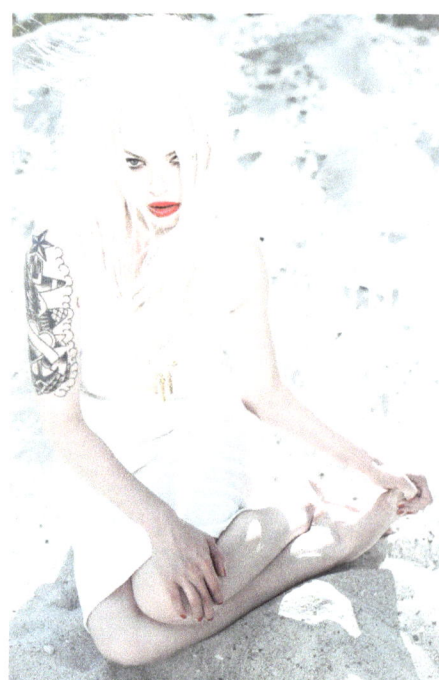

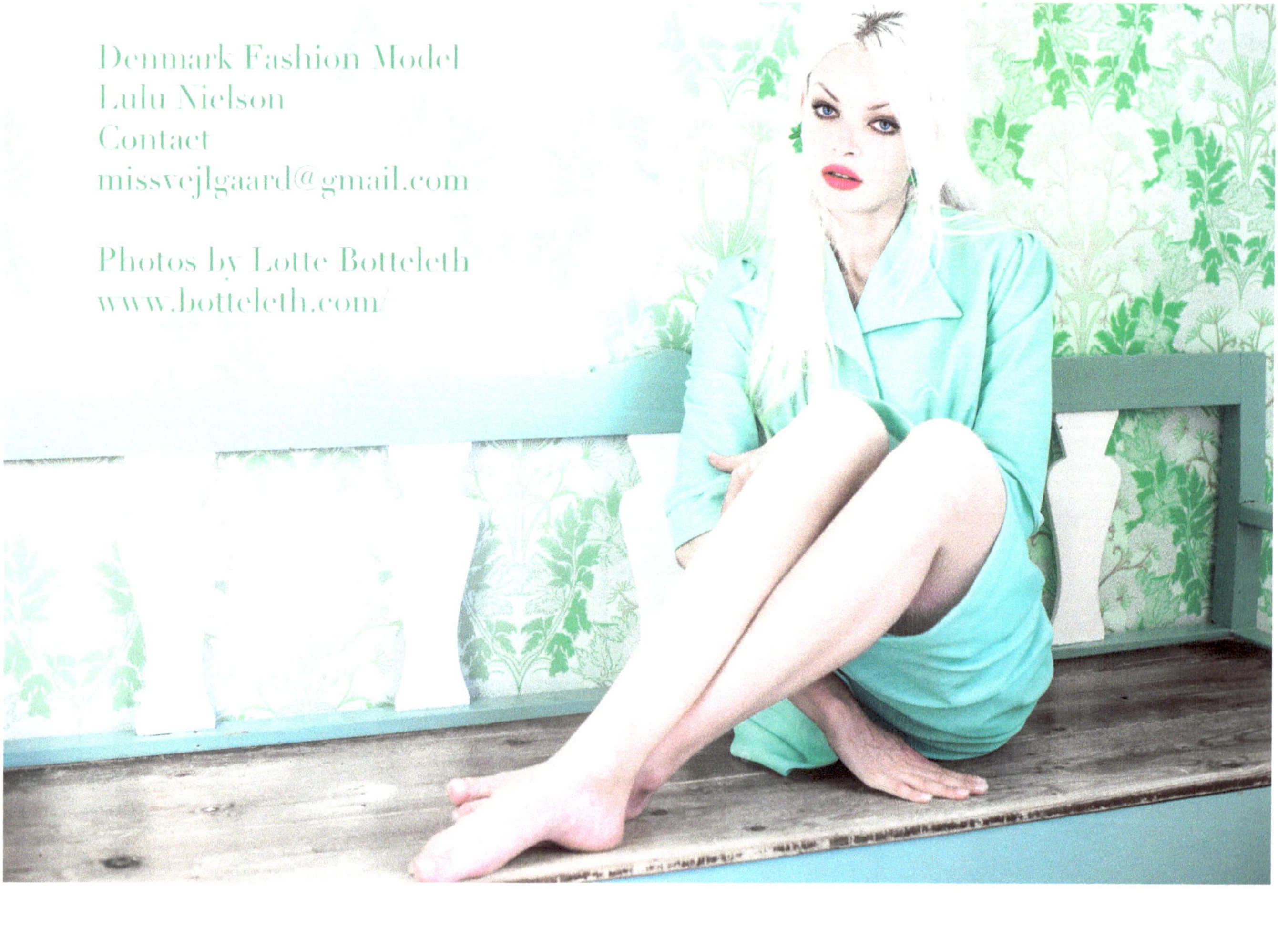

Denmark Fashion Model
Lulu Nielson
Contact
missvejlgaard@gmail.com

Photos by Lotte Bottcleth
www.bottclcth.com

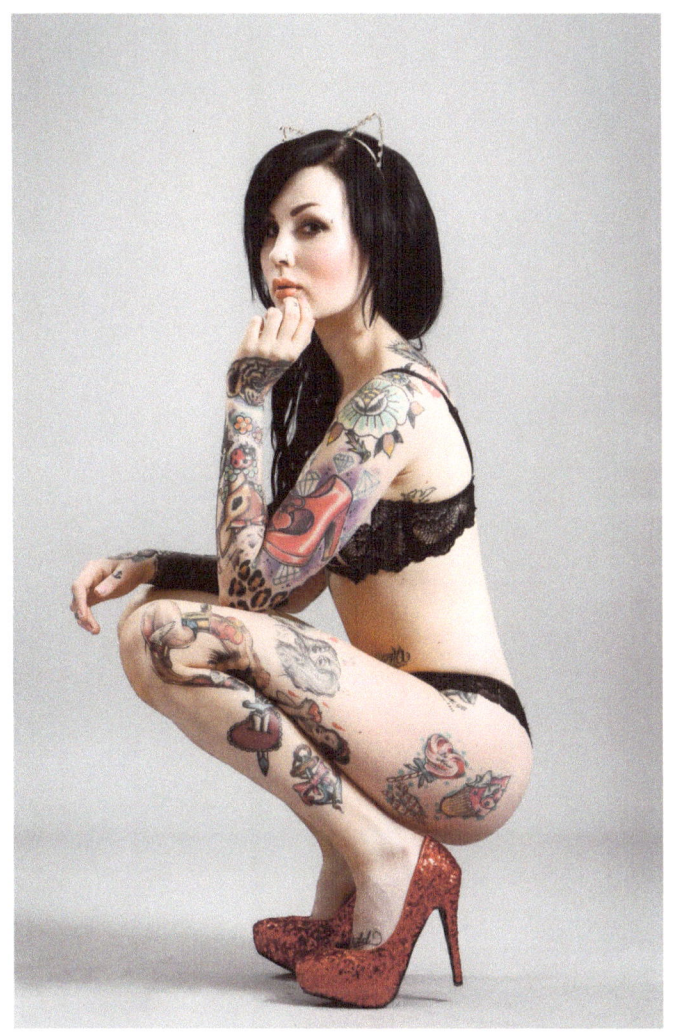

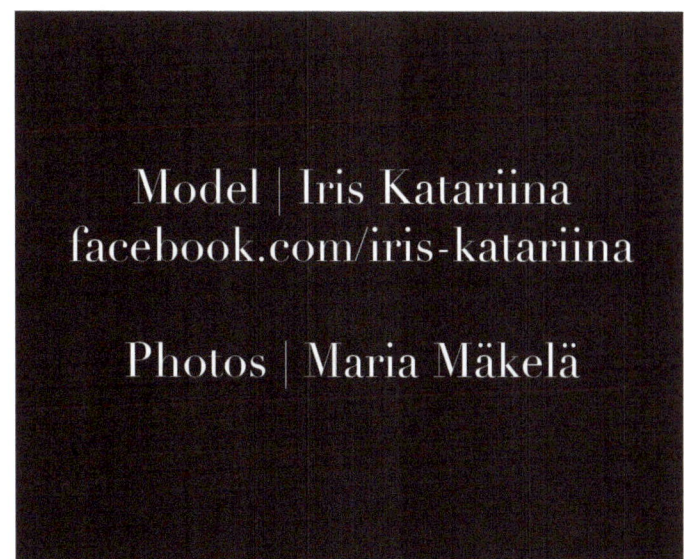

Model | Iris Katariina
facebook.com/iris-katariina

Photos | Maria Mäkelä

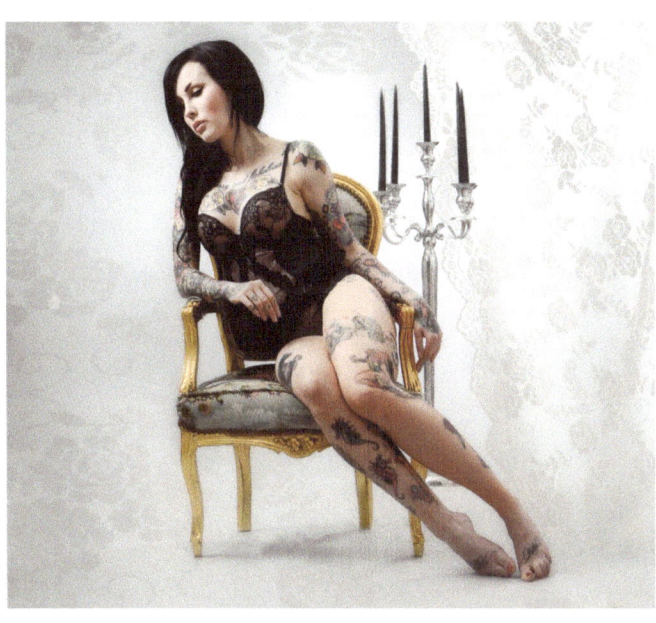

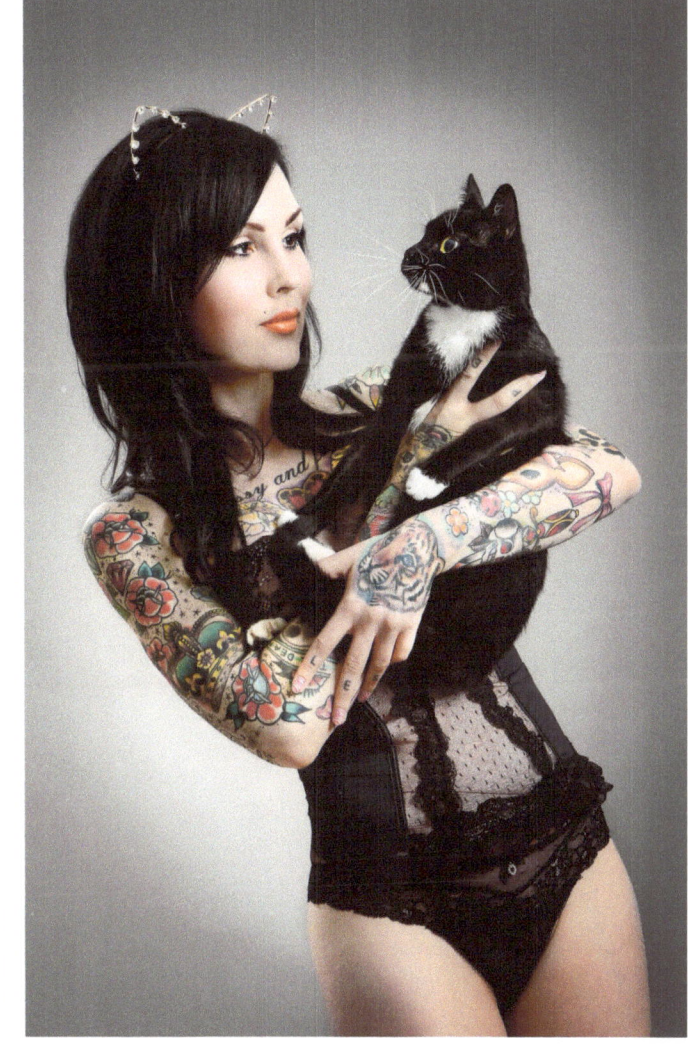

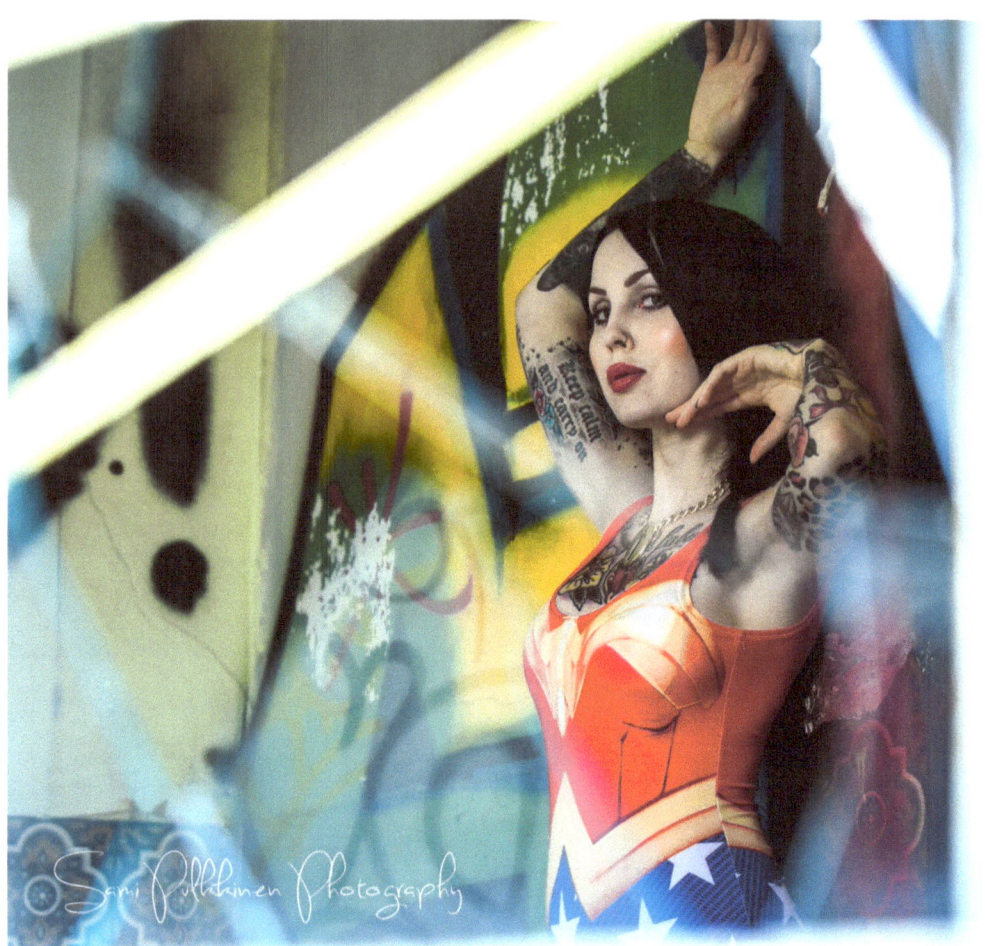
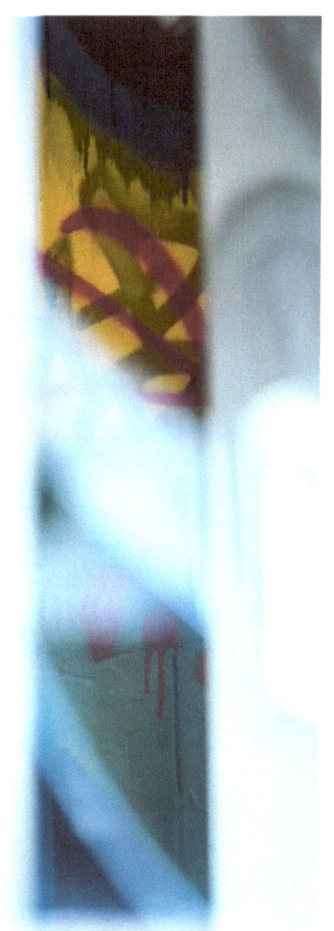

Model | Iris Katariina
facebook.com/iriskatariinaFI

Photos | Sami Pulkkinen
www.samipulkkinen.com

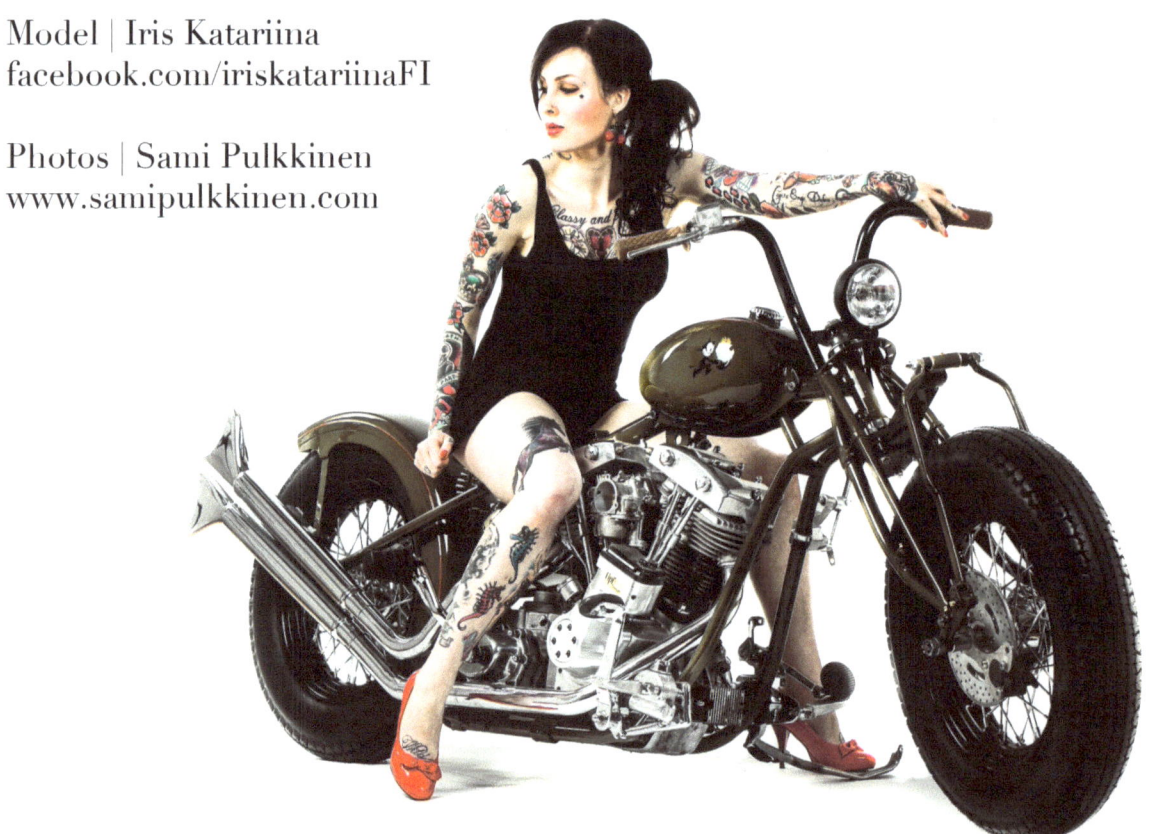

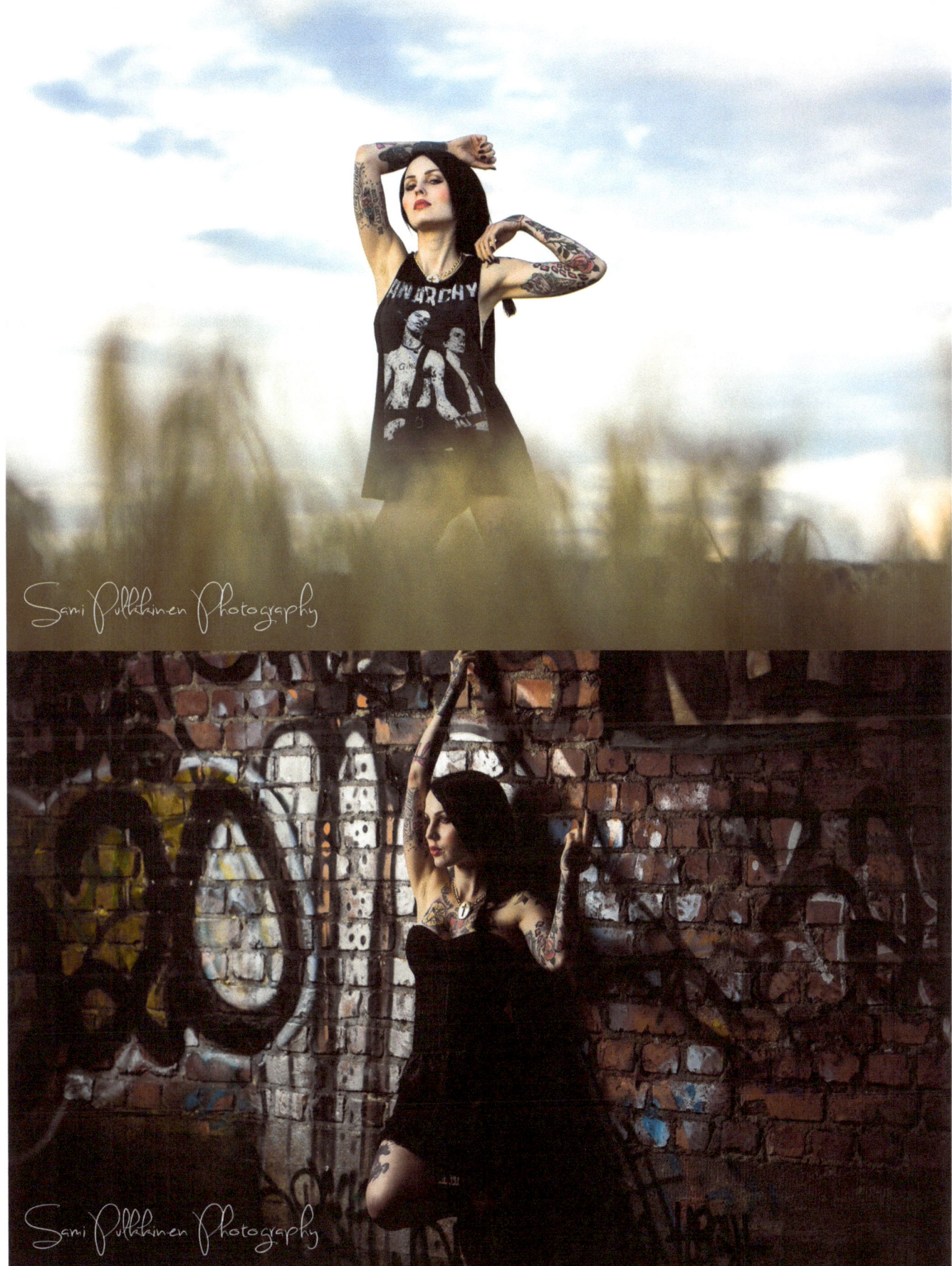

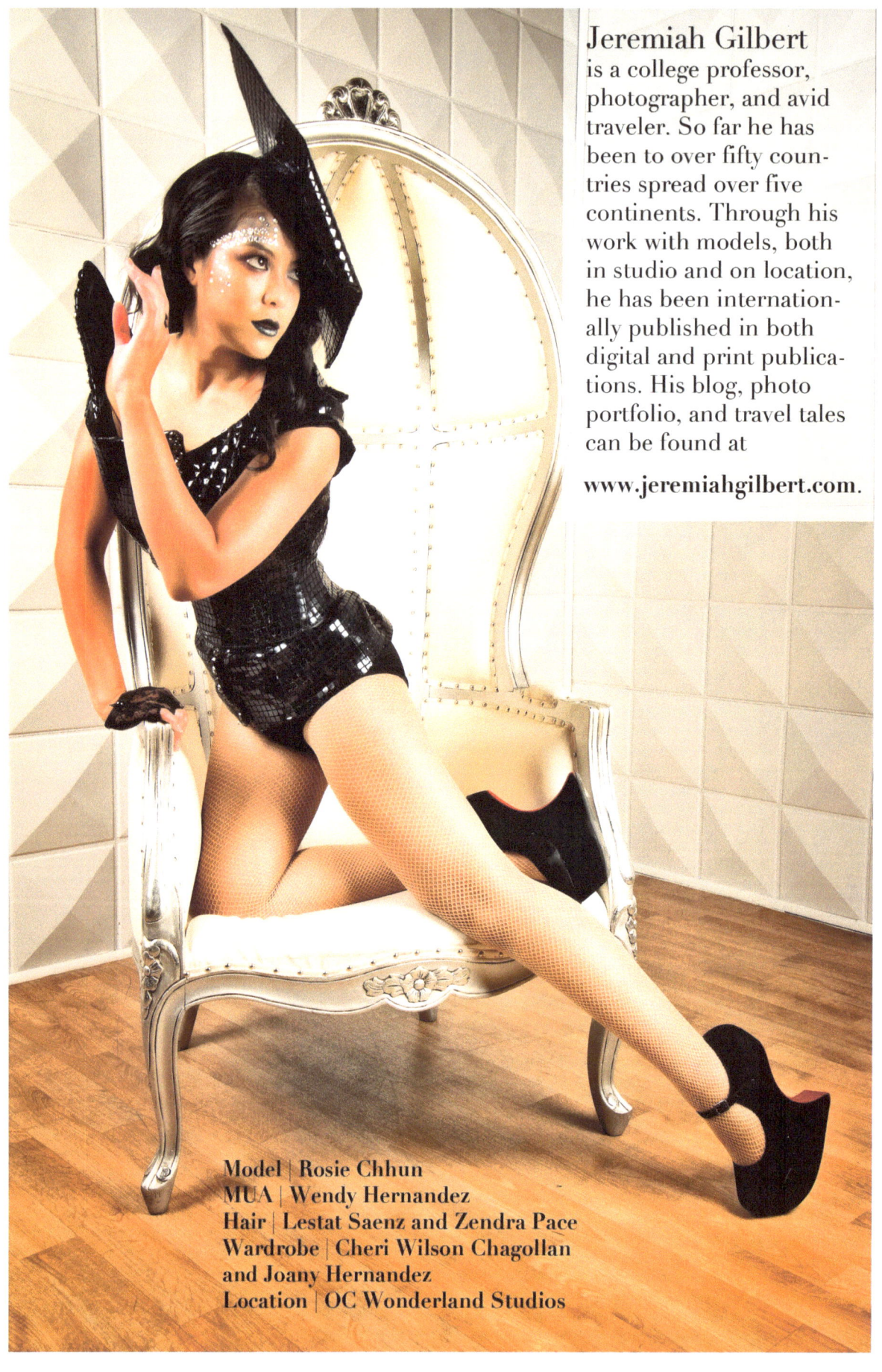

Jeremiah Gilbert is a college professor, photographer, and avid traveler. So far he has been to over fifty countries spread over five continents. Through his work with models, both in studio and on location, he has been internationally published in both digital and print publications. His blog, photo portfolio, and travel tales can be found at

www.jeremiahgilbert.com.

Model | Rosie Chhun
MUA | Wendy Hernandez
Hair | Lestat Saenz and Zendra Pace
Wardrobe | Cheri Wilson Chagollan
and Joany Hernandez
Location | OC Wonderland Studios

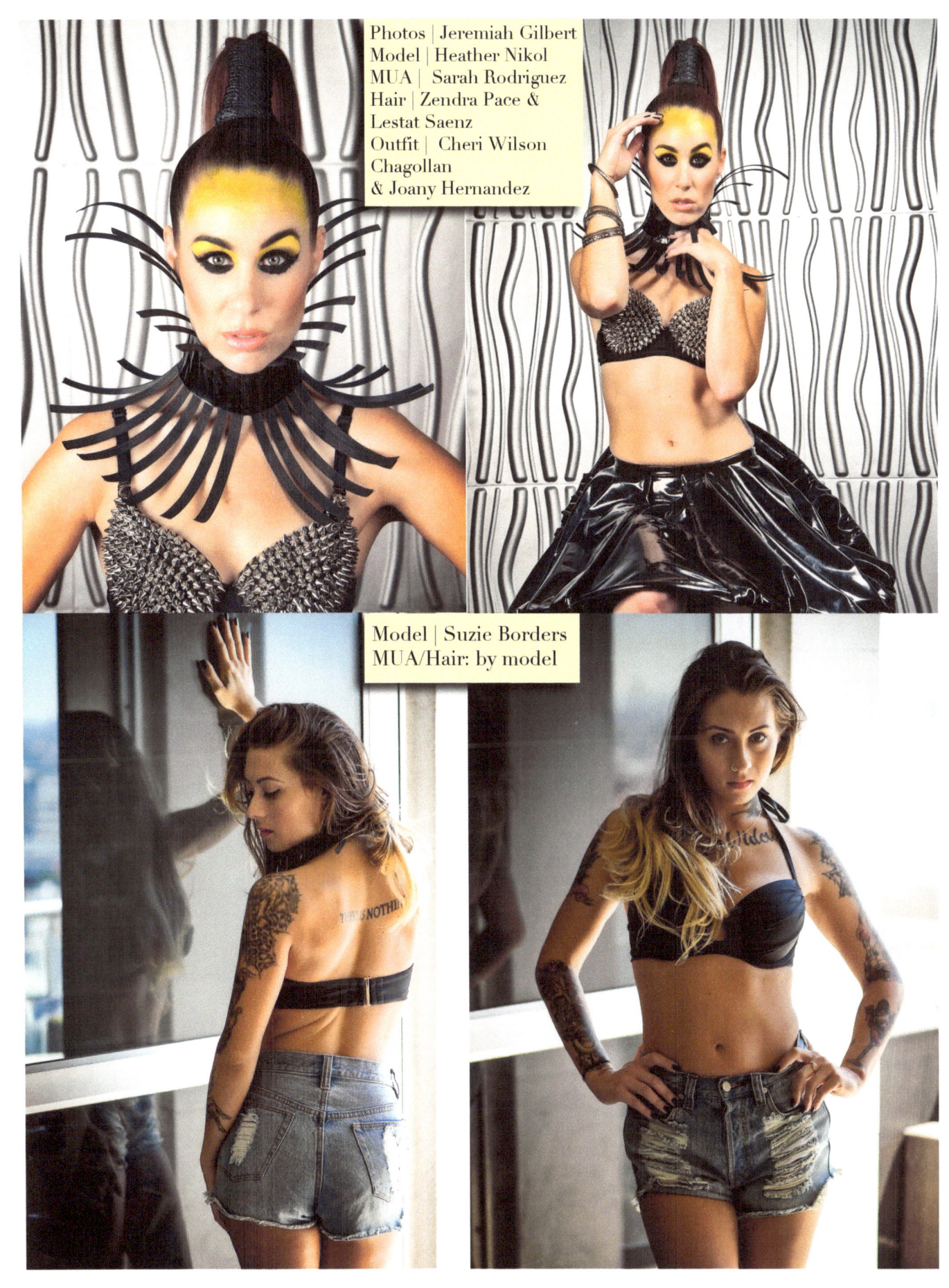

Photos | Jeremiah Gilbert
Model | Heather Nikol
MUA | Sarah Rodriguez
Hair | Zendra Pace &
Lestat Saenz
Outfit | Cheri Wilson
Chagollan
& Joany Hernandez

Model | Suzie Borders
MUA/Hair: by model

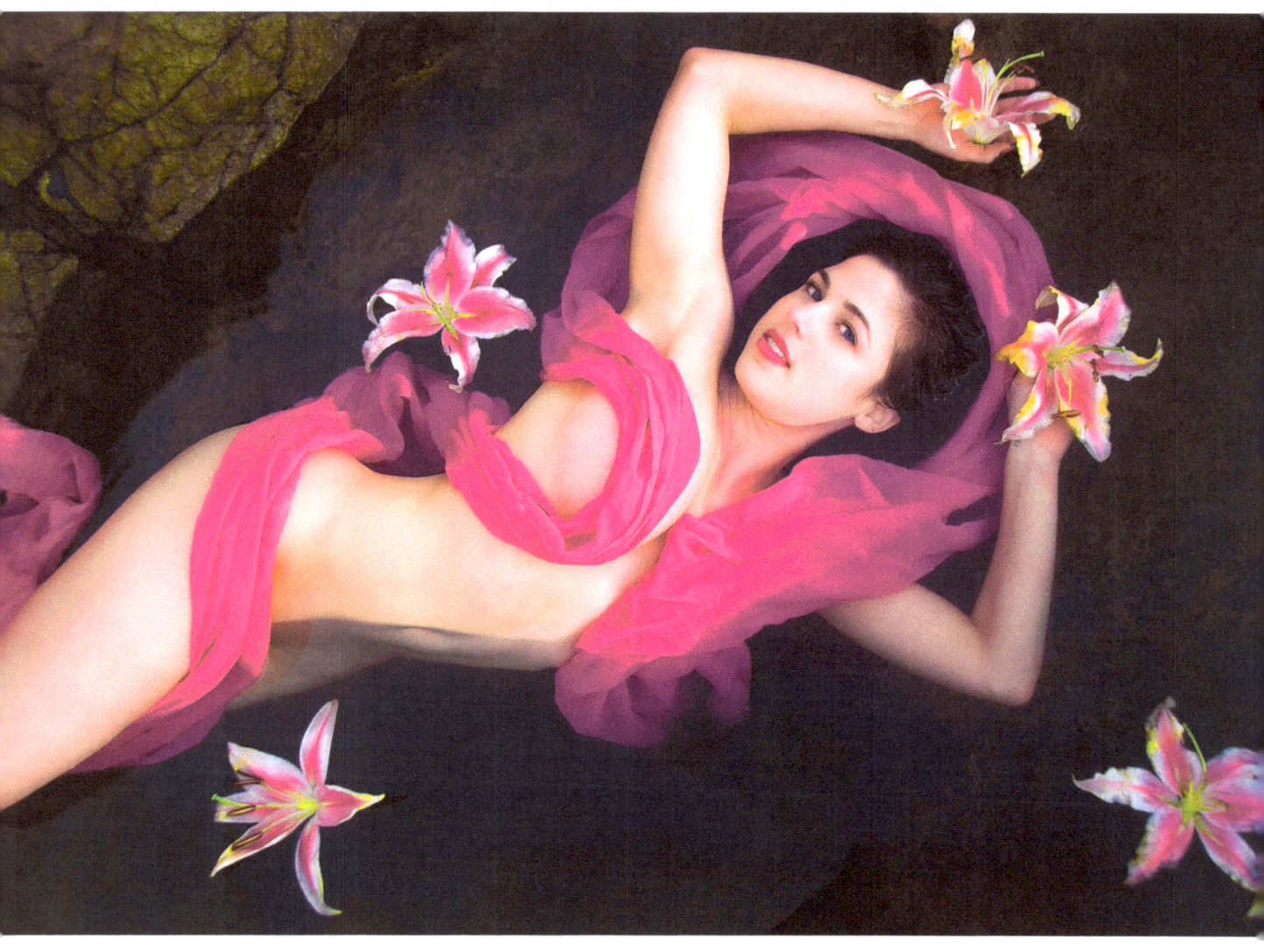

LA Model | Miss Hedy La Fleurt
IG @misshedylafleurt

Photo by Russ West Photography
modelmayhem.com/1796907

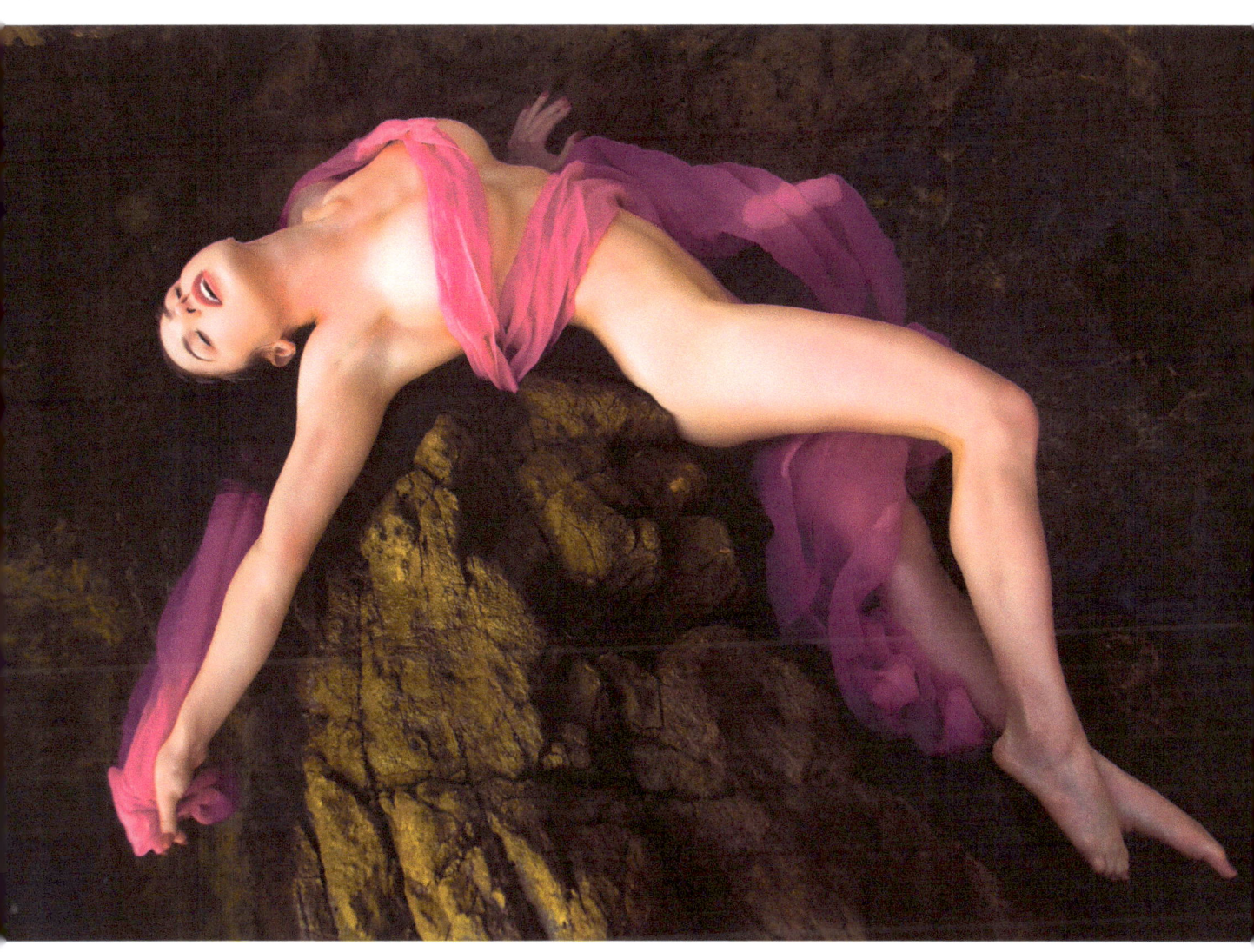

FROM THE DARK ROOM
FEATURED PHOTOGRAPHER, RICKY DAVIS

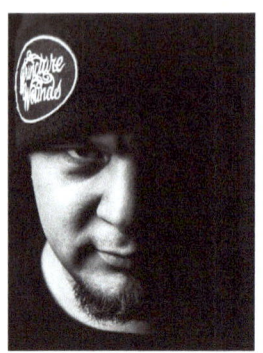

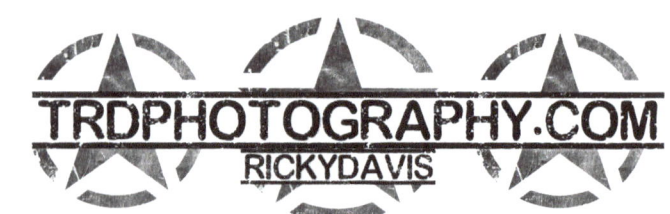

Ricky Davis, aka TRD Photography has been shooting professionally for several years now. Ricky says, "To be successful in a creative field, you have to be driven and you have to be your own worst critic. You can't look at the others that work in your local area and just think about where your work stands against theirs, you have to find the best out there and figure out how to get your work there. It's a life-long process in my opinion and that's what will make your work standout. You have to be original; don't ever be a carbon copy of someone else. " These are just a few lessons Ricky has learned along the way.

What Ricky is most passionate about is his work in the alt scene. "It's a different culture and I just find myself and my vision fitting this genre the best. I love getting to work with such artistic and creative people. It's been an interesting journey for me, especially this year, as I really began to take my faith a lot more seriously and that has become the driving force behind what I do. It's made me re-evaluate my motivation and what I'm willing to put out there, but it's also been really cool because I've been able to really connect with people on a different level," says Ricky.

Ricky is based in the Chattanooga, Tennessee area but is willing to travel wherever the clients are interested. "I really am a sucker for black and white work, but I really dig colorful in your face attitude type work as well as artistic concept type stuff. I hate getting locked into a specific style as I get bored somewhat easy and like to keep it fresh," says Ricky. If you're interested in checking out more of Ricky's work you can connect with him at the following.

www.facebook.com/trdphotography
Instagram - @trd_photography
Twitter - @trd_photography
Website – www.trdphotography.com

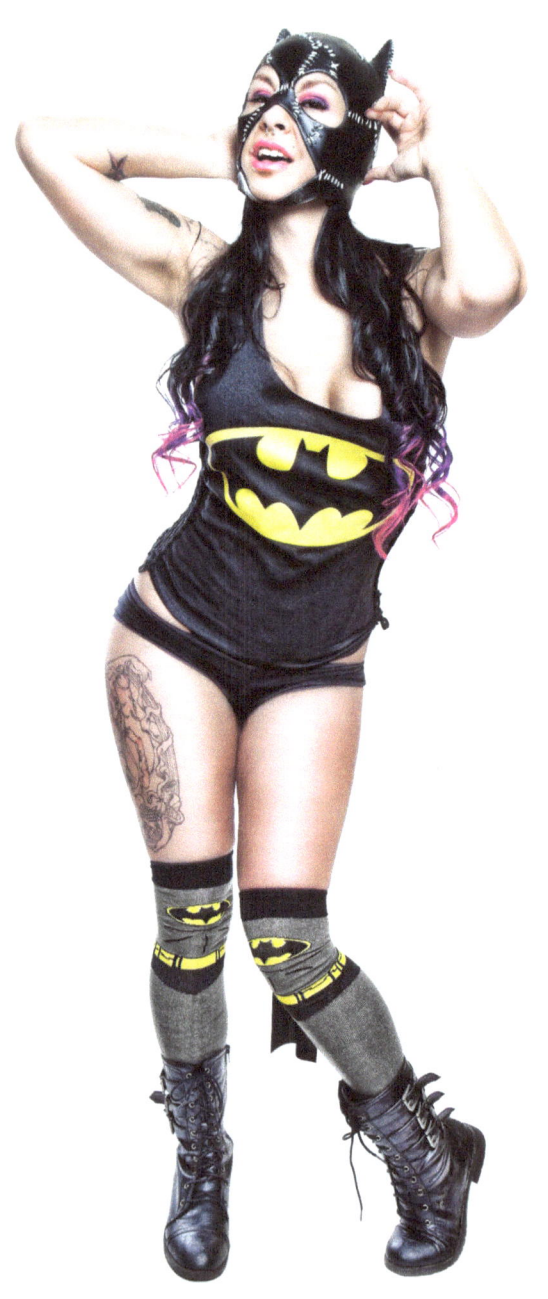

Model | Vanessa Michelle
www.facebook.com/VanessaMichelleFilth
Instagram @filthfamily

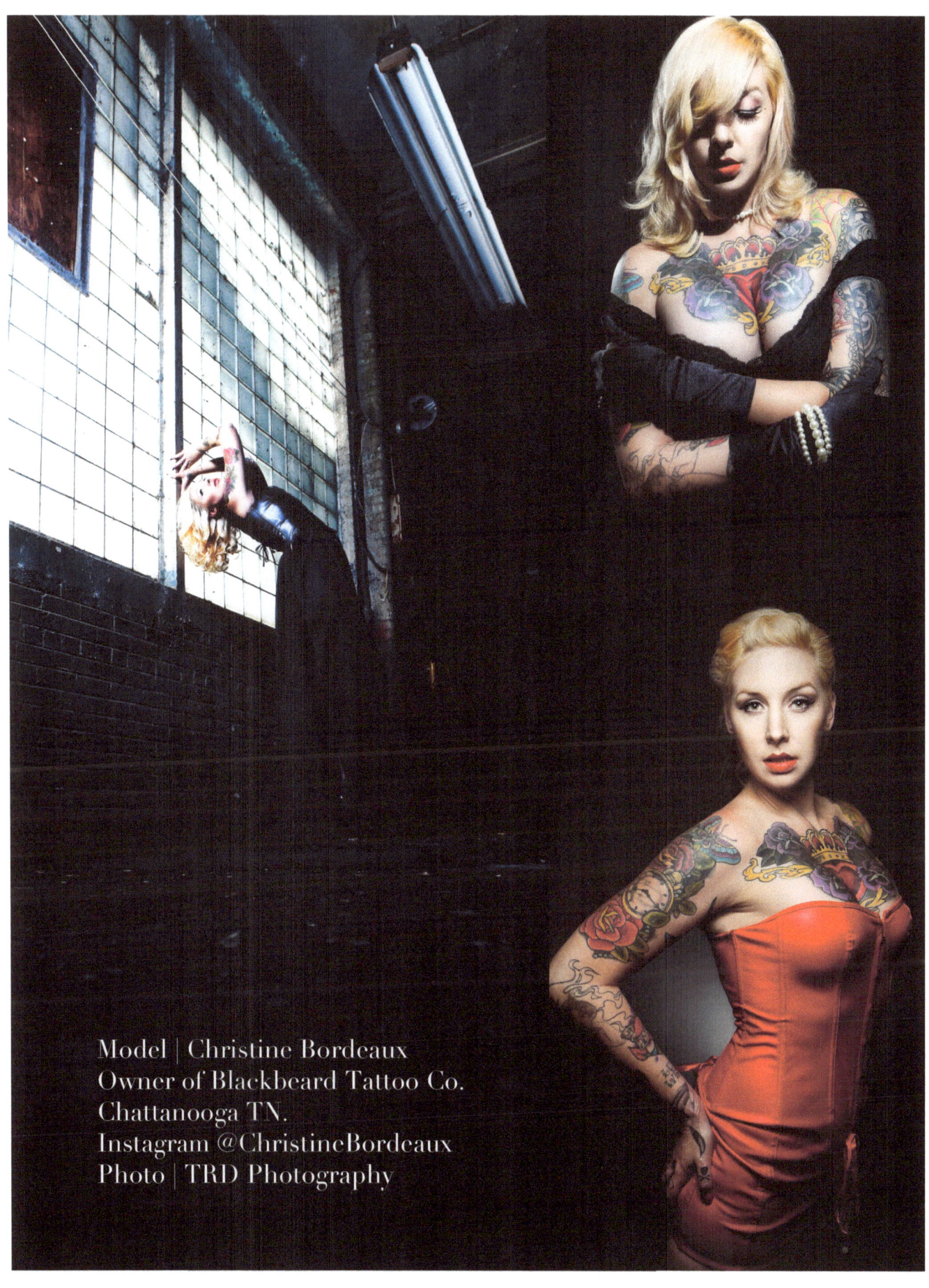

Model | Christine Bordeaux
Owner of Blackbeard Tattoo Co.
Chattanooga TN.
Instagram @ChristineBordeaux
Photo | TRD Photography

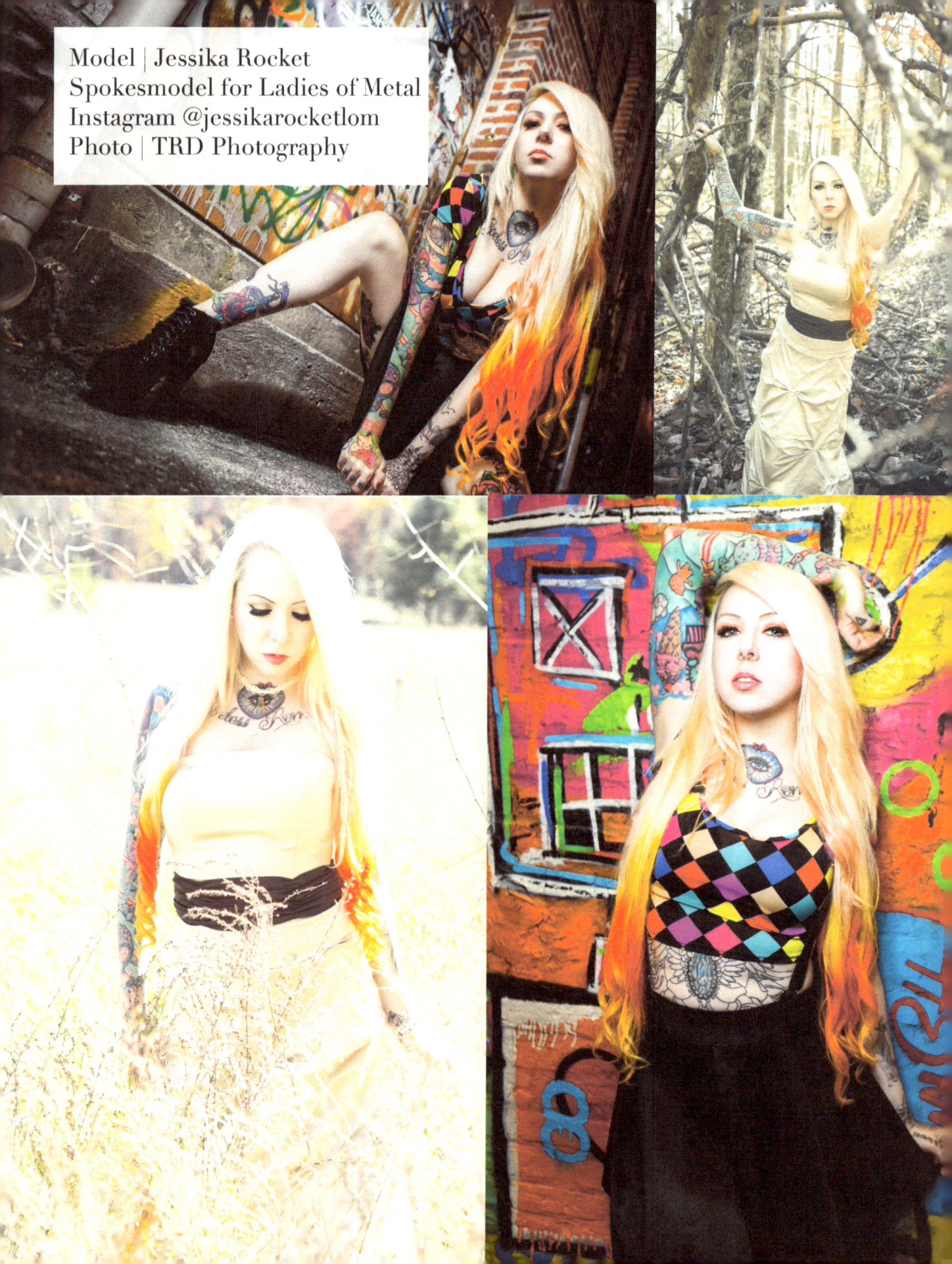

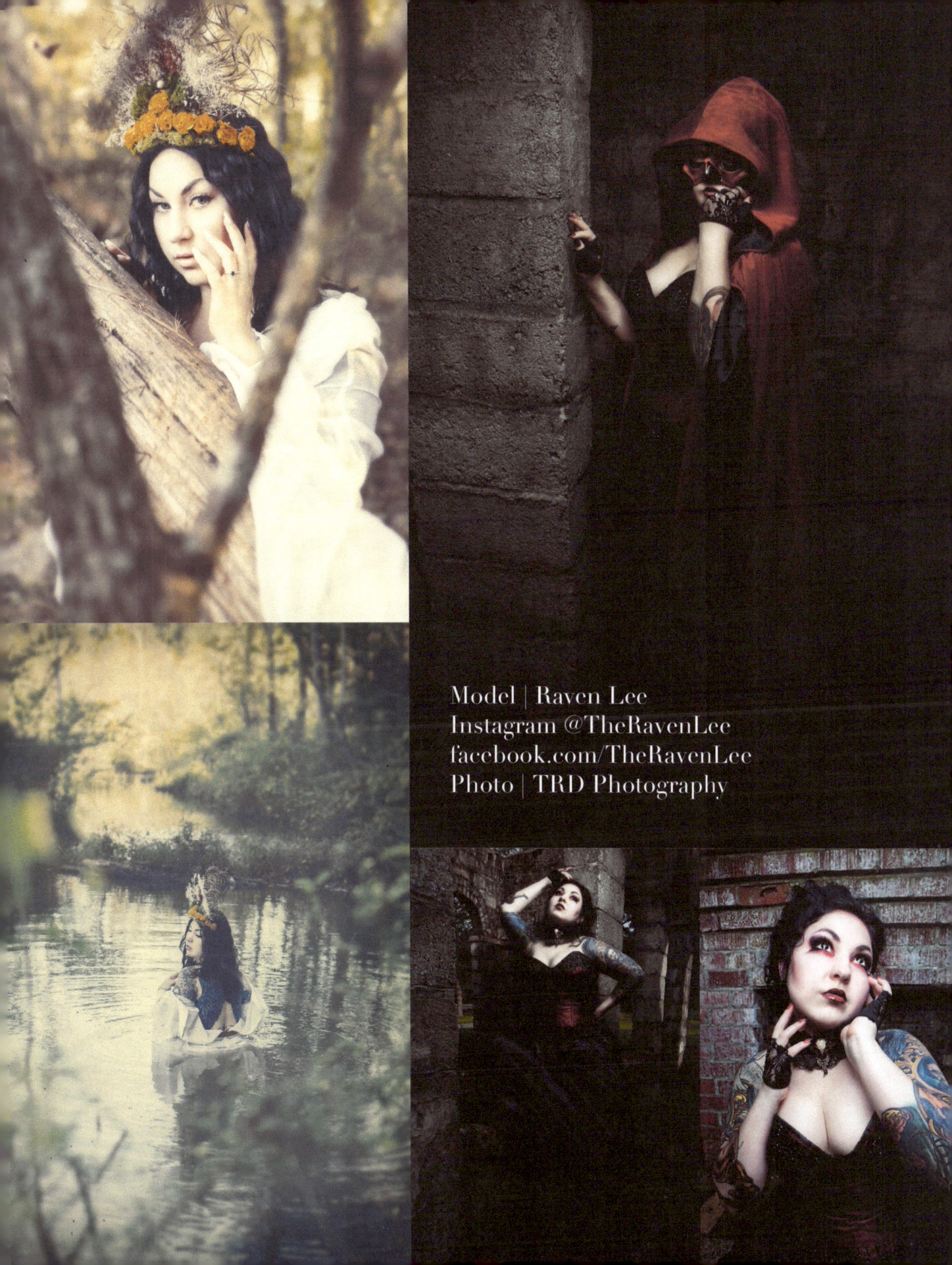

Model | Raven Lee
Instagram @TheRavenLee
facebook.com/TheRavenLee
Photo | TRD Photography

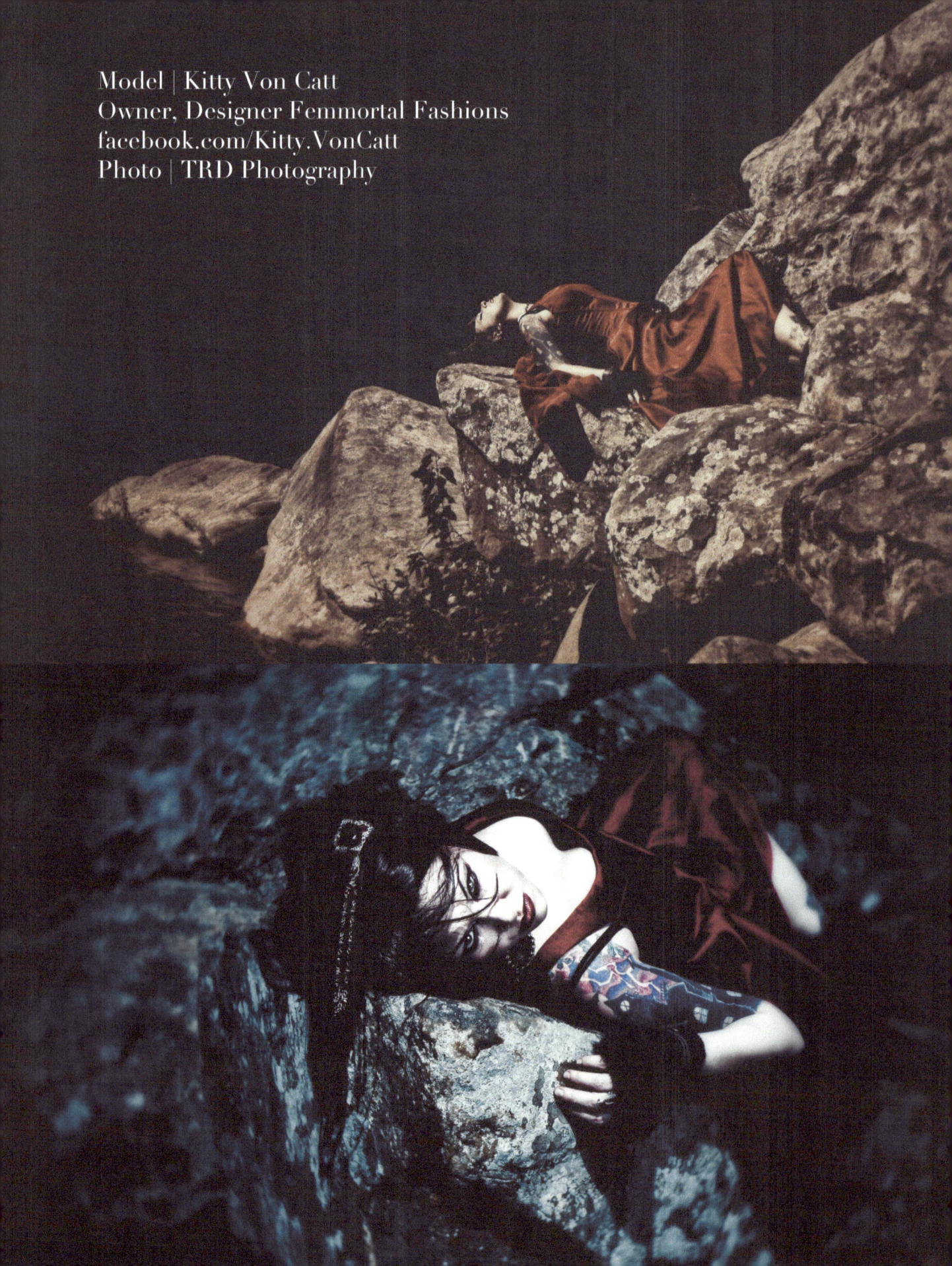

Model | Kitty Von Catt
Owner, Designer Femmortal Fashions
facebook.com/Kitty.VonCatt
Photo | TRD Photography

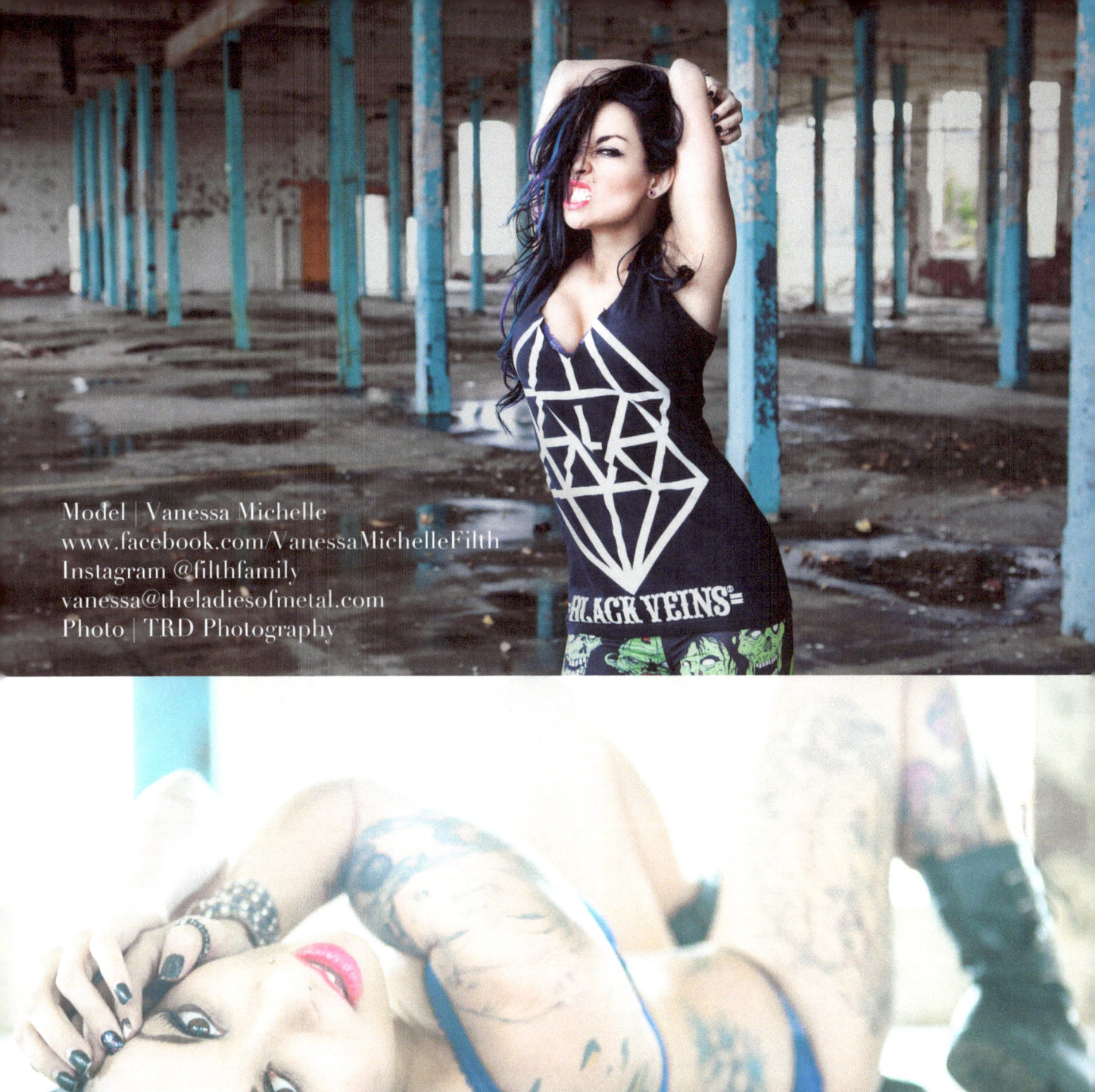

Model | Vanessa Michelle
www.facebook.com/VanessaMichelleFilth
Instagram @filthfamily
vanessa@theladiesofmetal.com
Photo | TRD Photography

Prince Pat

Patrick Nguyen aka **Prince Pat**, was born and raised in Orange County and has loved art since he opened his first comic which was a very old issue of *Fantastic Four*. After studying fine arts and graphic design with an Associate's at Santa College and a Bachelor's from Cal State Fullerton, he painted full time while freelancing as a designer. Patrick fell in love with photography when he picked up his first camera which was a Cannon Rebel tiı, and is fascinated with Pin-Up and fashion photography. "My goal is to forcibly shove my artistic flair into my photography works and always try to improve as an artist." says Patrick. To see more of Patrick's work visit

www.princepat.com
IG @princepat3ooo

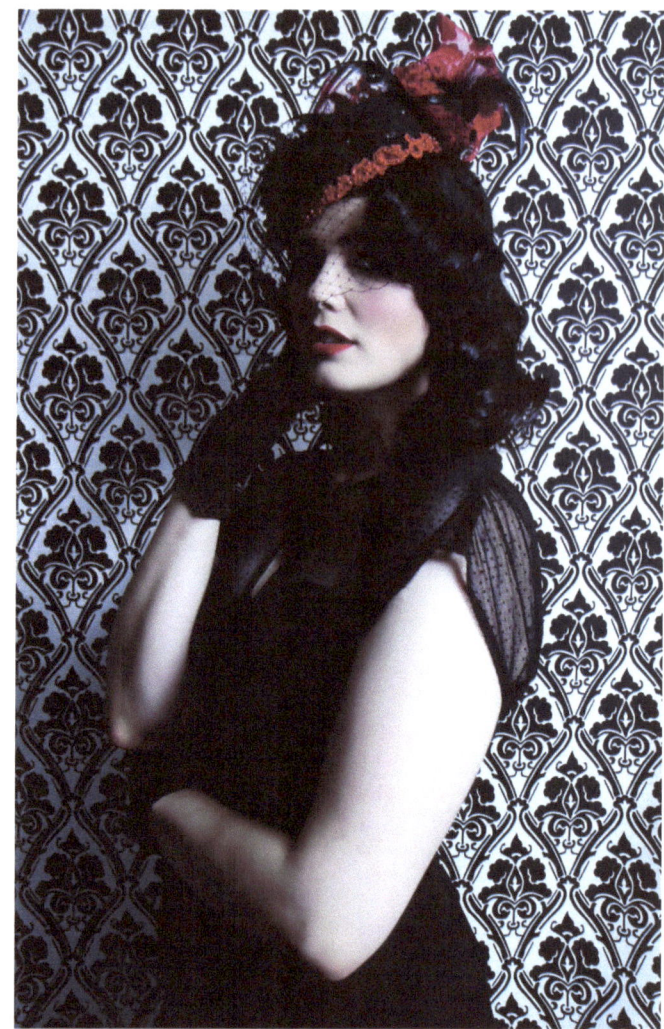

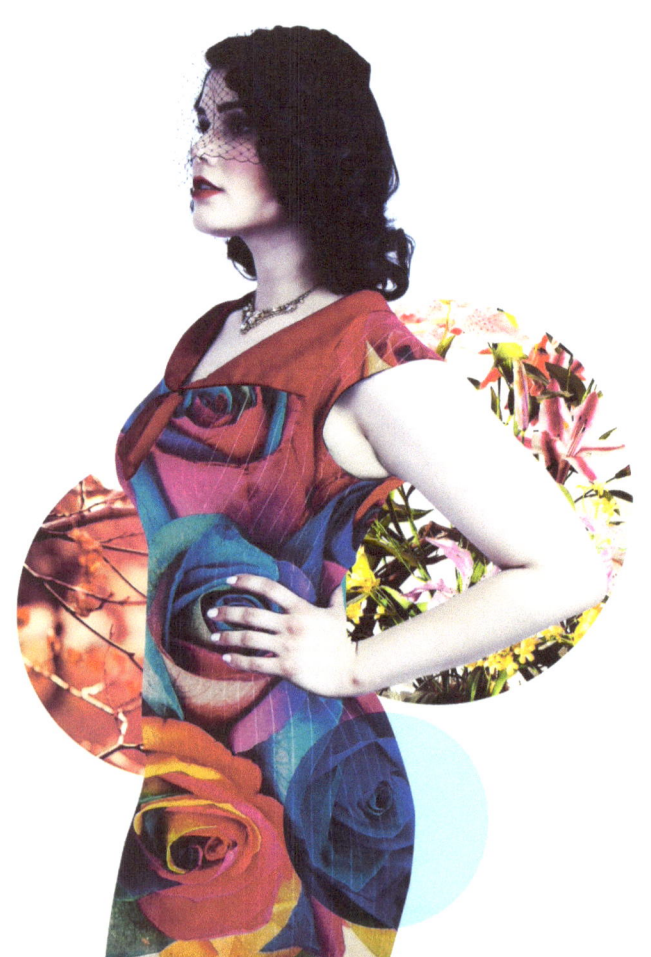

Model | Katherine Dresser
facebook.com/katiescarlettcosplay
IG @katiescarlettcurtains

I don't know much about Katie other than that she's cute and does a mean *Sailor Moon* and *Tardis* (Doctor Who) Cosplay. Katie describes herself as, "Curtain clothier. Butt Charmer. Potential Slayer. Triwizard runner-up. Heartless Guttersnipe." That sounds like someone I'd like to get to know better.

SIN FISTED

A California native based out of Los Angeles, SIN has over 16 years of experience & she knows what it takes to put on an unforgettable show. Starting off in bikini bars, she quickly made a name for herself & changed the way we see exotic dancing today. She paved the way for "alternative" dancers as well as pole dancers & has helped mold pole dancing into what it was intended to be: An art form & a sport.

Her professionalism goes above and beyond & with her reputation as "easy to work with, flexible, reliable & insanely punctual", she is doing repeat events with producers from coast to coast & internationally.

There is Nothing that can stop this woman! She is loyal & completely dedicated to giving you THE BEST performance experience possible, no matter what.

Her looks are ever evolving, this woman is a complete chameleon. And with such a wide variety of different performances, it makes her great to book all year round! From sultry & sexy to violent & dangerous- Look no further, you have found what you were looking for!

(source) www.sinfisted.com   18+ content

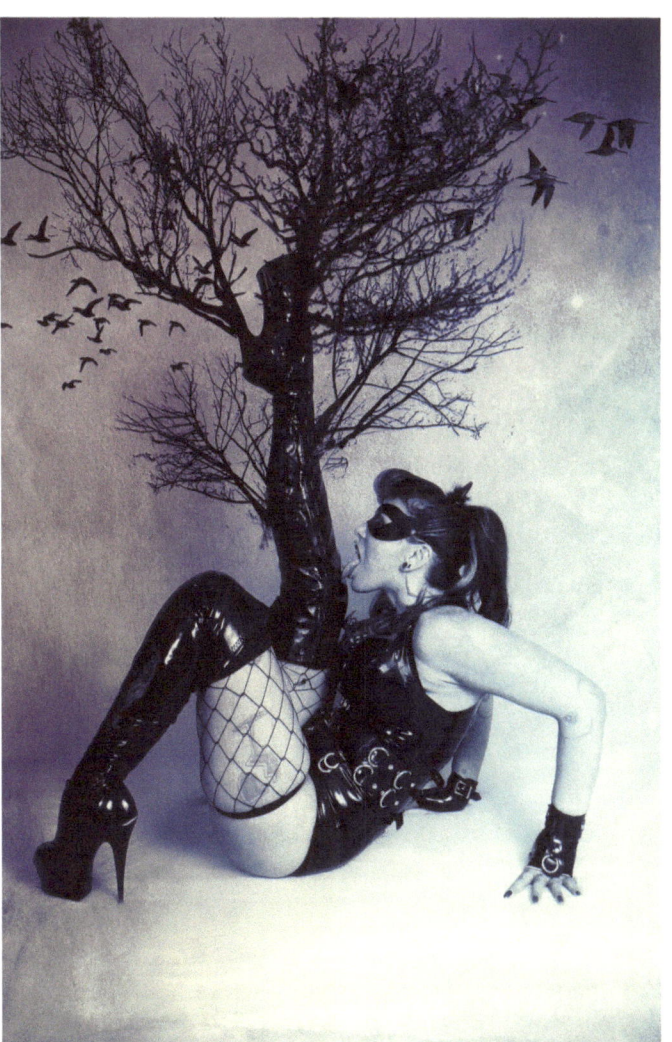

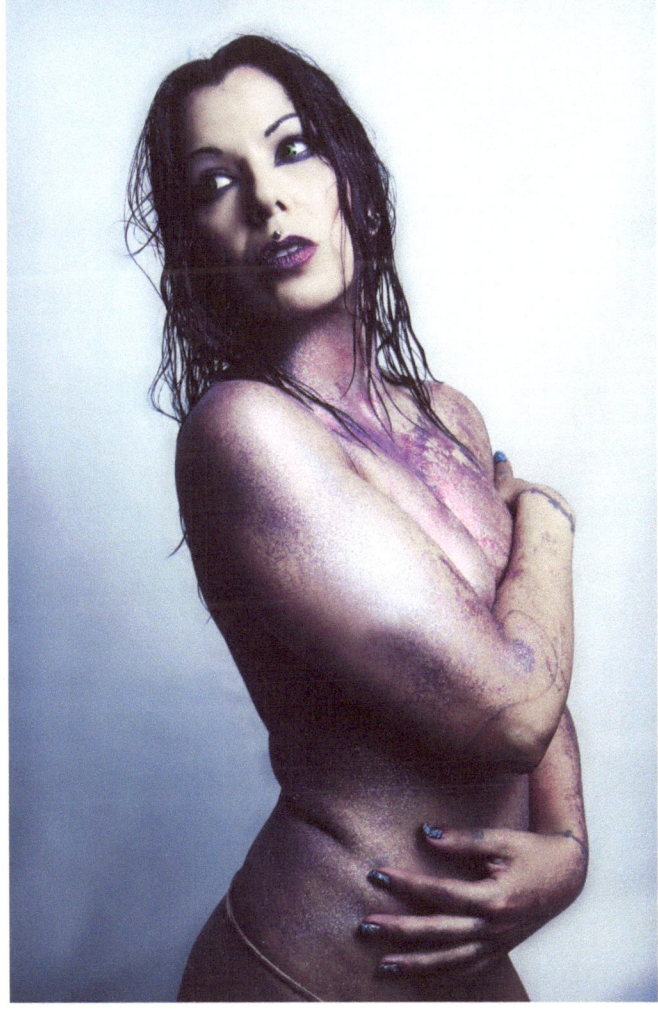

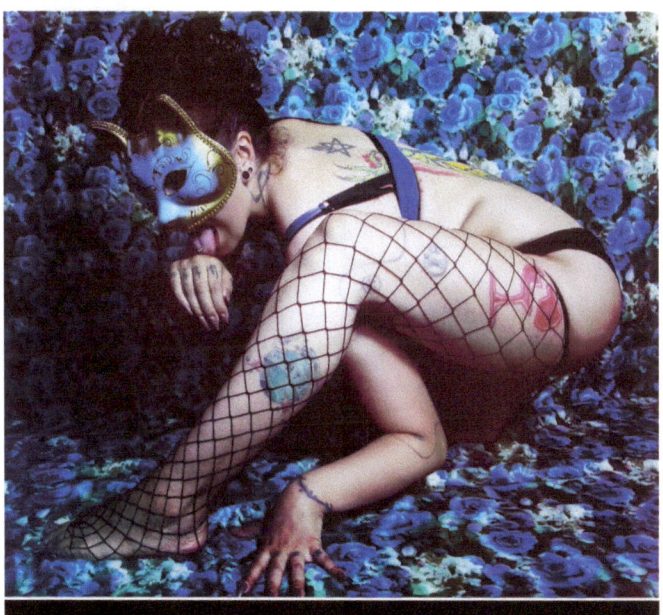

Photos | Prince Pat | www.princepat.com
Model | Sin Fisted | www.sinfisted.com

Photo | S.H. Photo

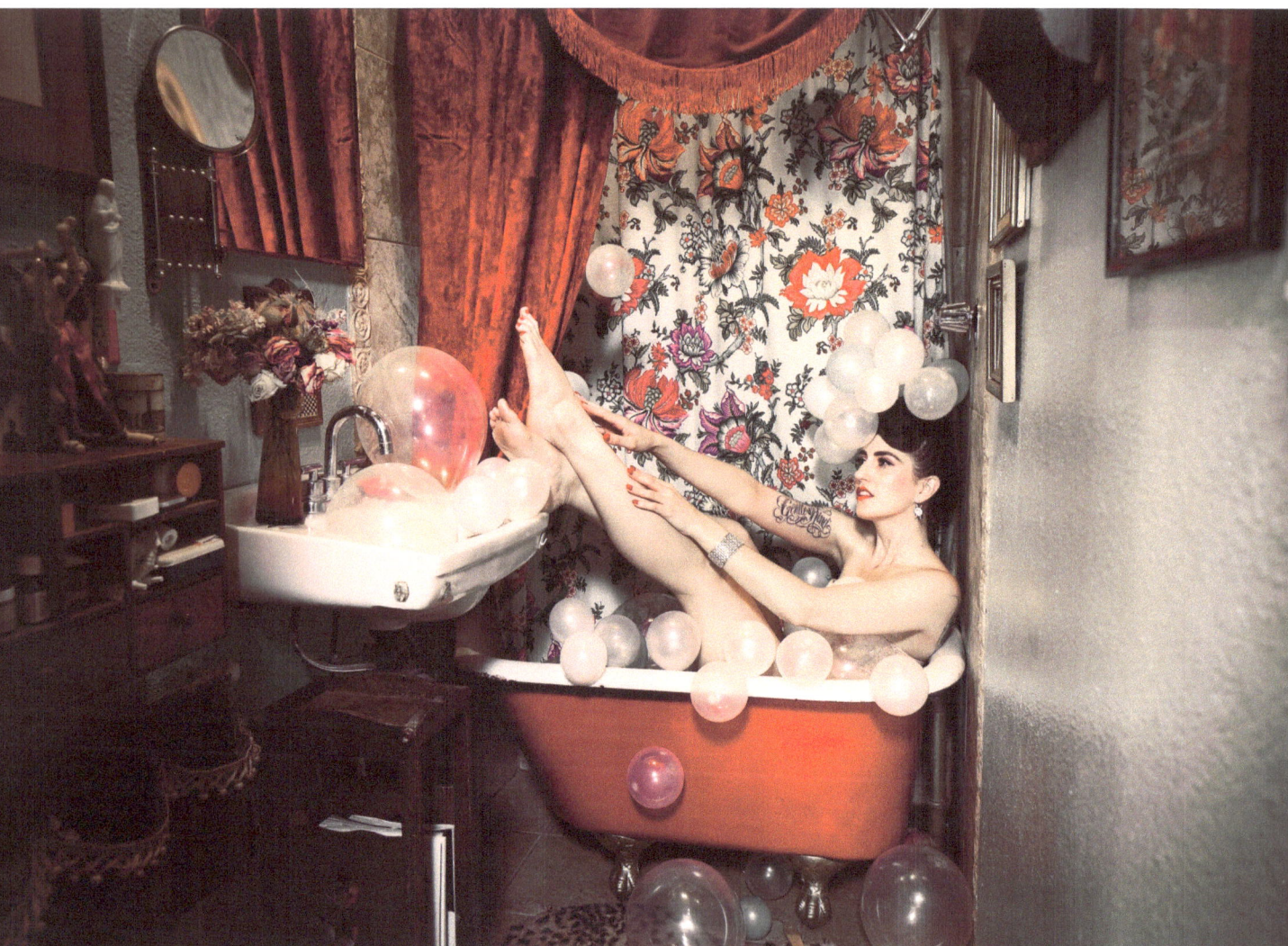

Based in Los Angeles, Sam Hernandez has shot everything from the Emmys and pro sports to corporate events, commercial catalogs and the Burlesque Hall of Fame. His strong work ethic, talent and personality have won him the respect of his models, many of whom consider him their favorite photographer. This shot was inspired by burlesque performer, Iza La Vamp's "Bubble Bath" routine, and shot in the bathroom of Marissa Gomez.

www.shphotolab.com

Model | Iza La Vamp

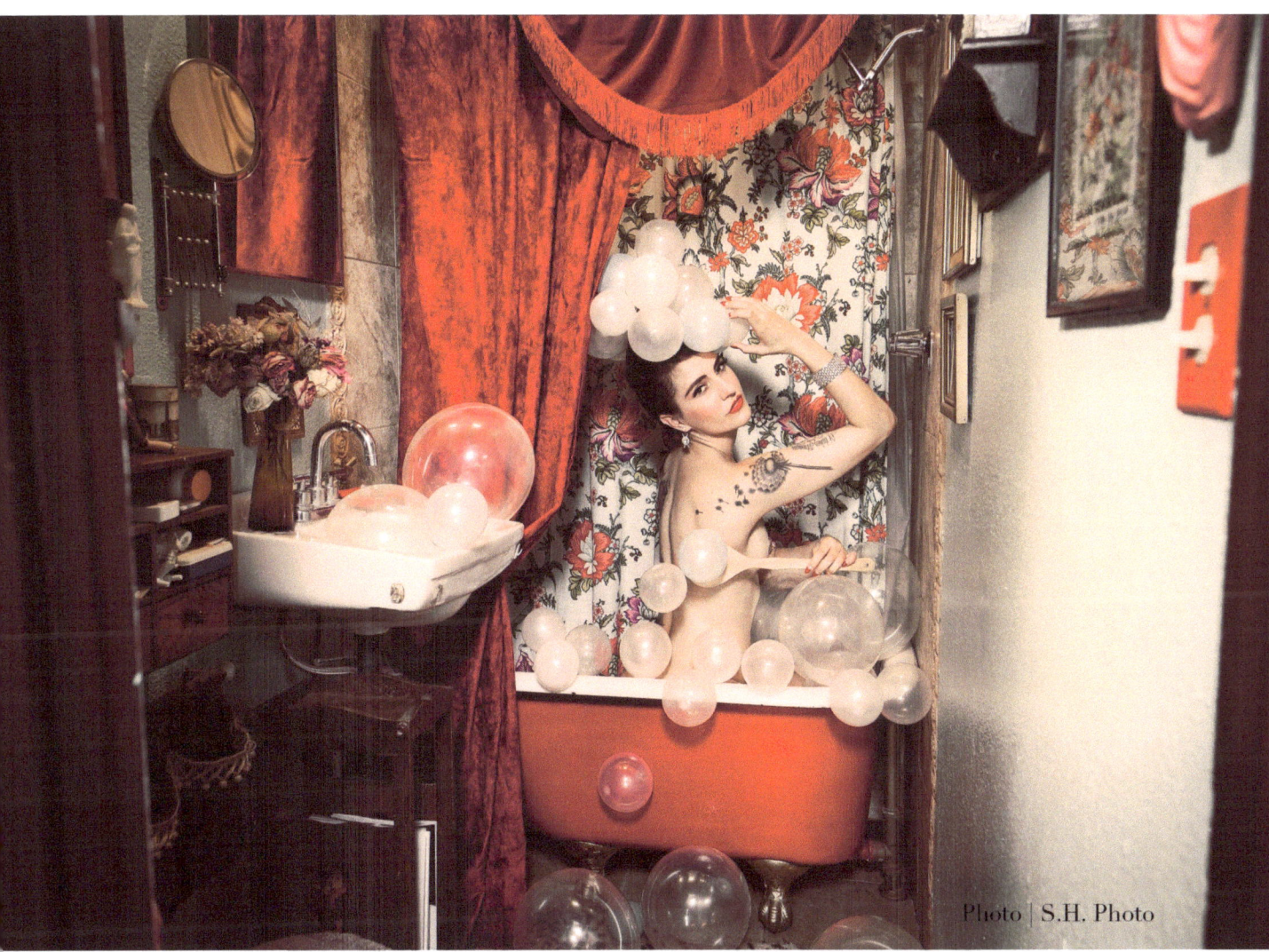

Photo | S.H. Photo

Iza la Vamp was a chorus girl on her way to center stage until a freak accident froze her body in a cryogenic freezer. Thankfully, she is now defrosted and ready to perform burlesque. She is finding herself in a different time with different music and history to catch up with. Join her on a burlesque adventure in recreating herself and making sense of all the changes she is encountering.

www.izalavamp.com

Photo | Trever Brandt
IG @tabmt
Model | Christina Darko
Instagram @van_darko_
Helena, Montana

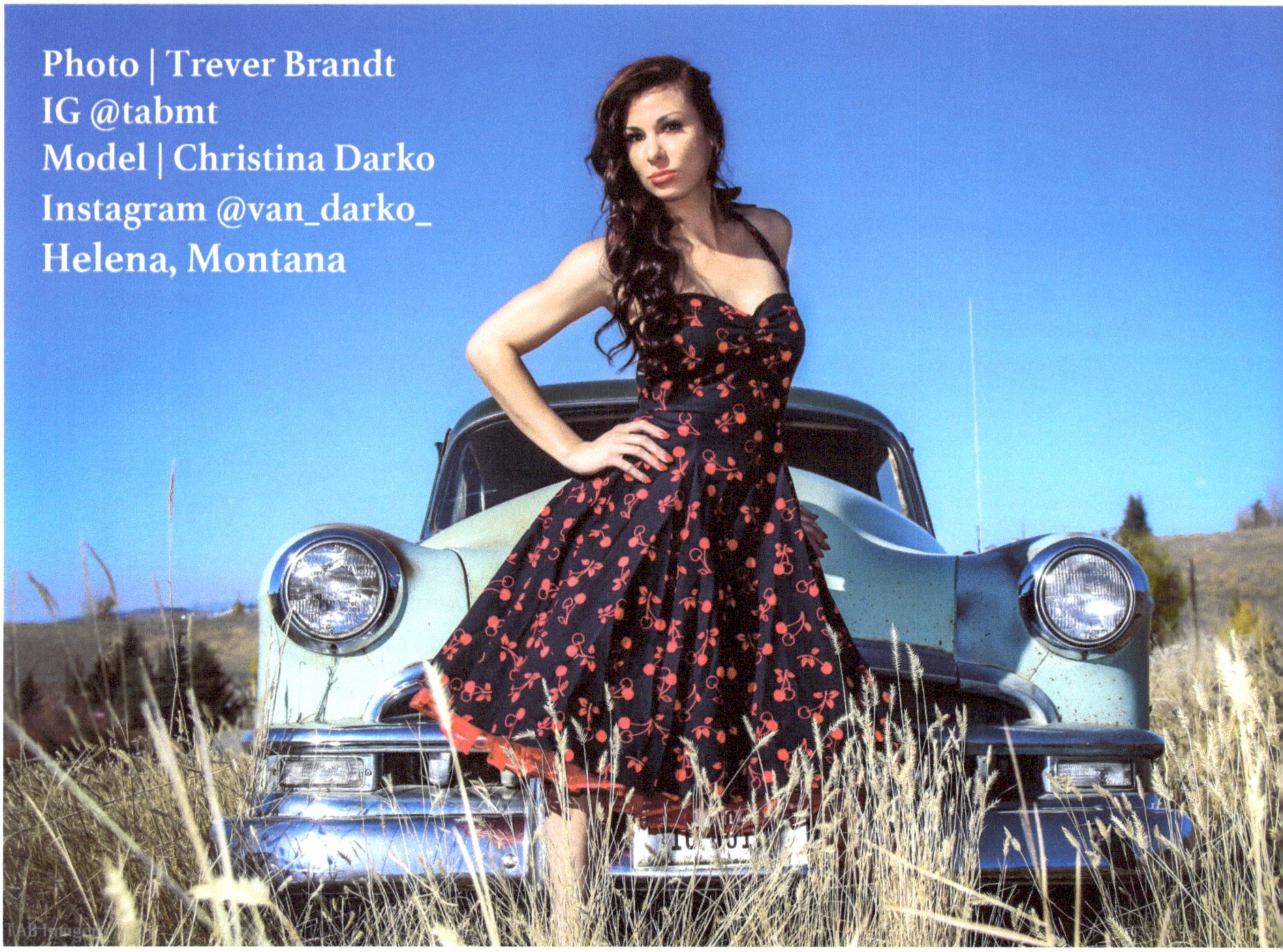

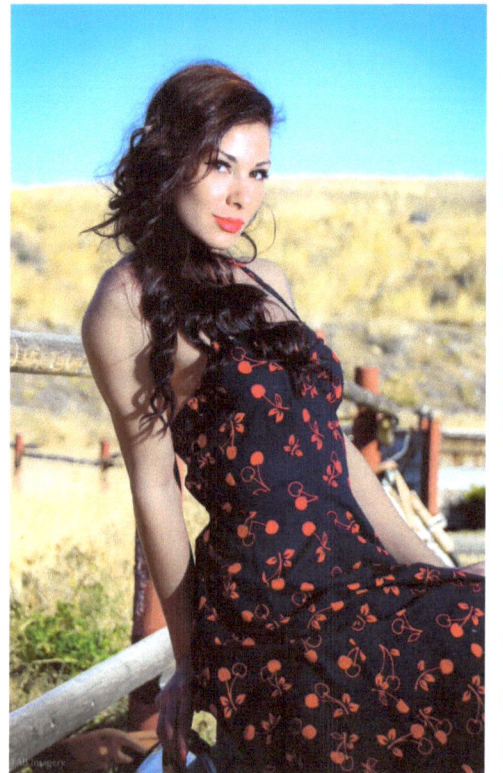

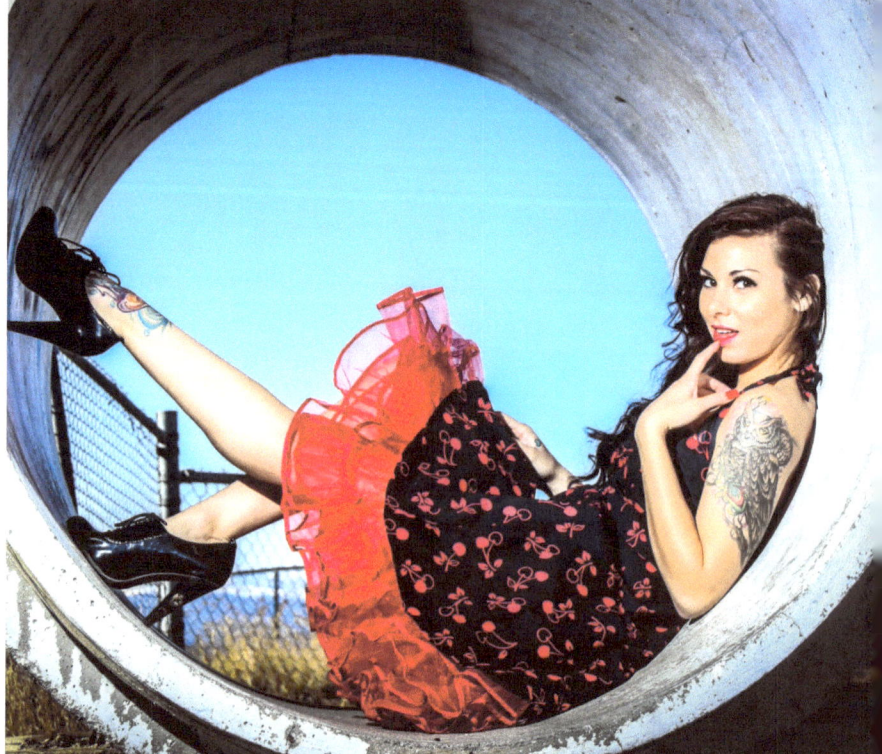

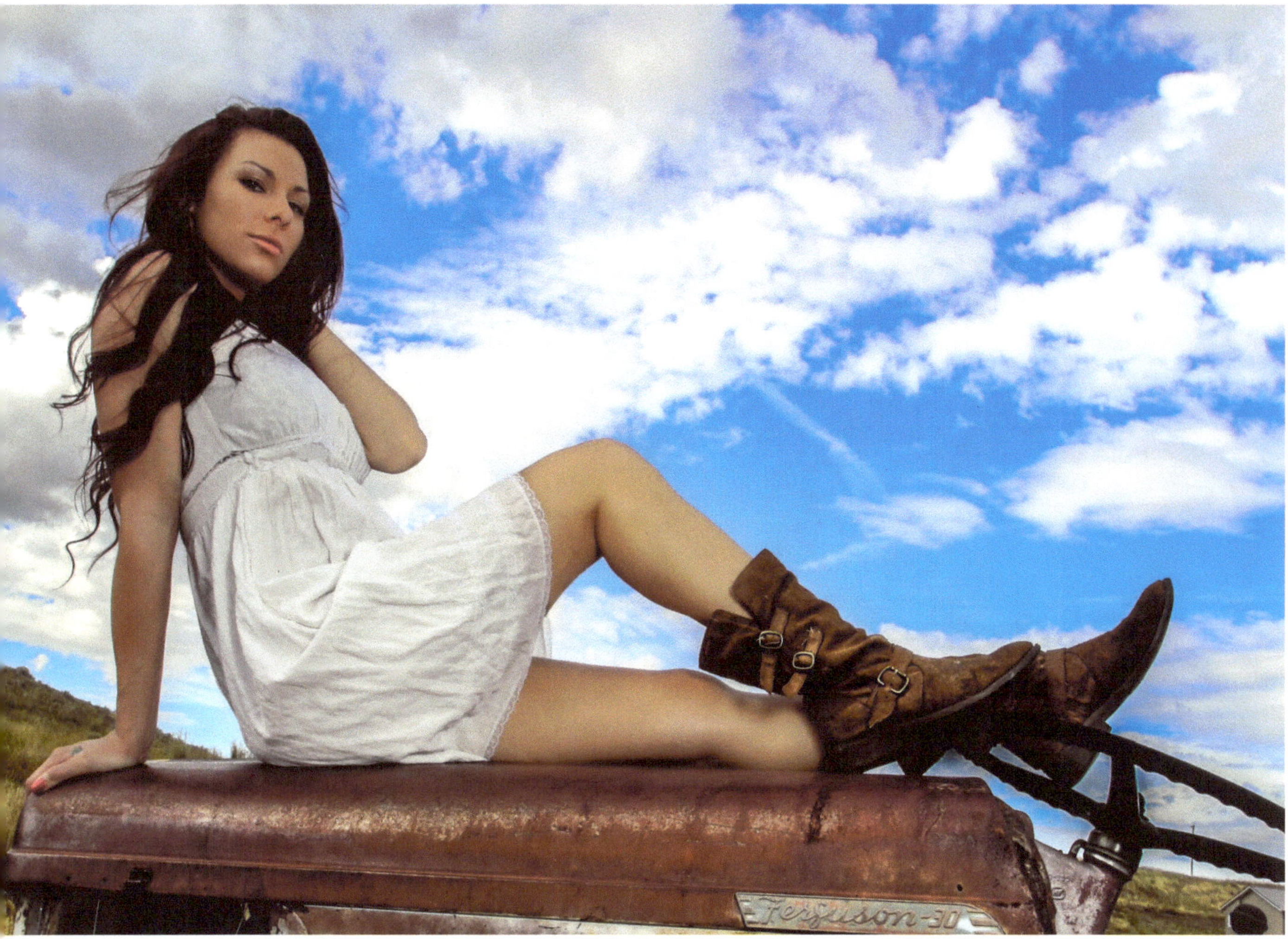

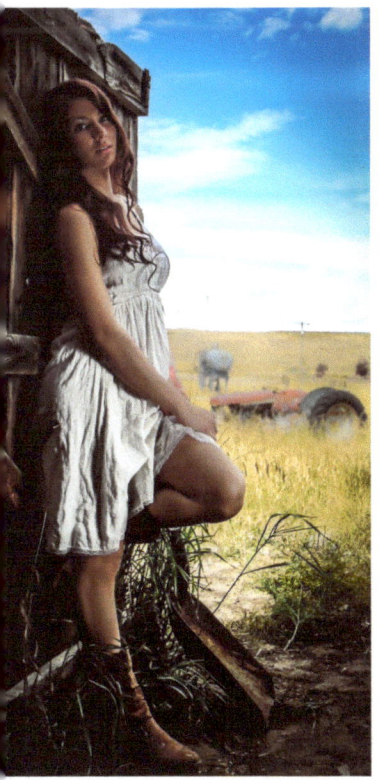
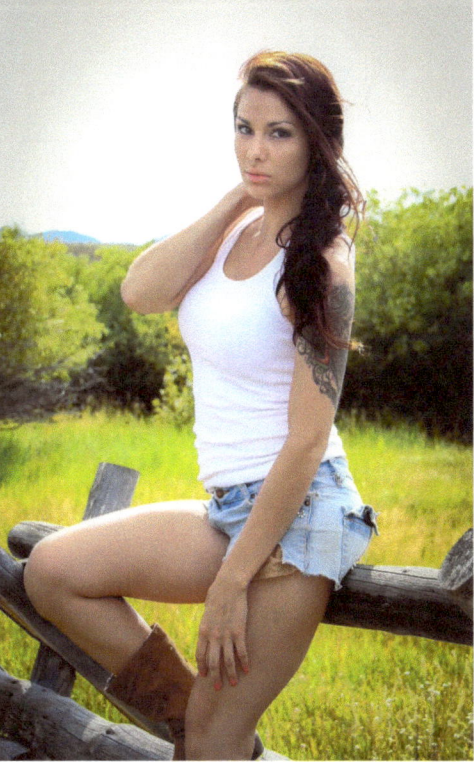
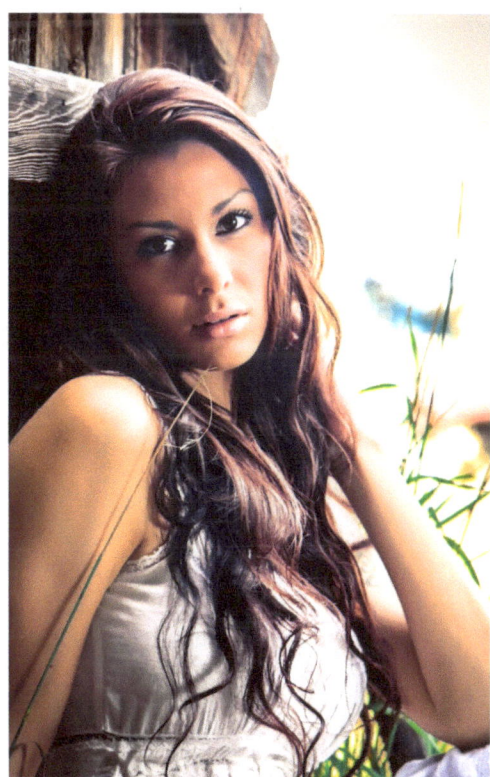

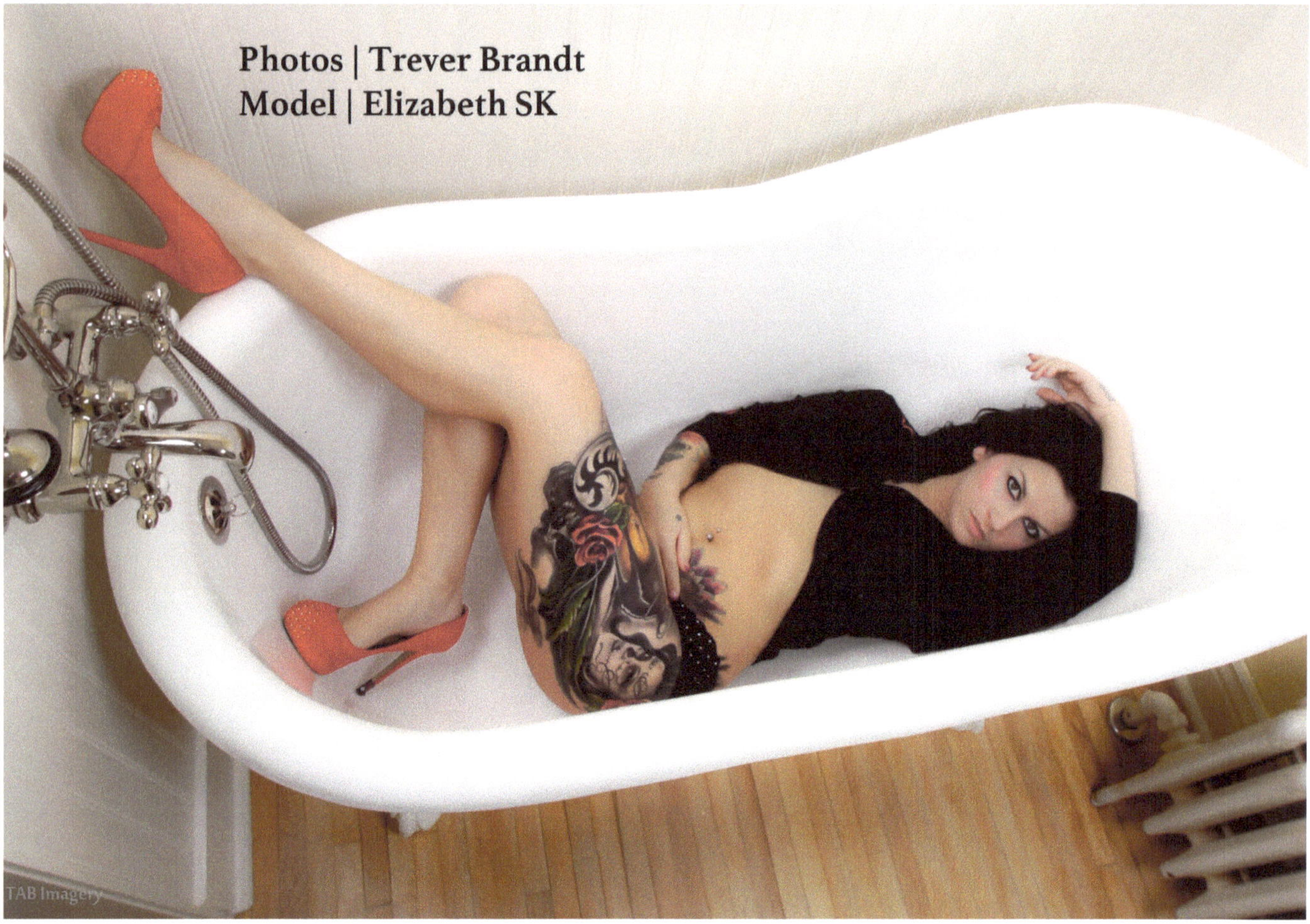

Photos | Trever Brandt
Model | Elizabeth SK

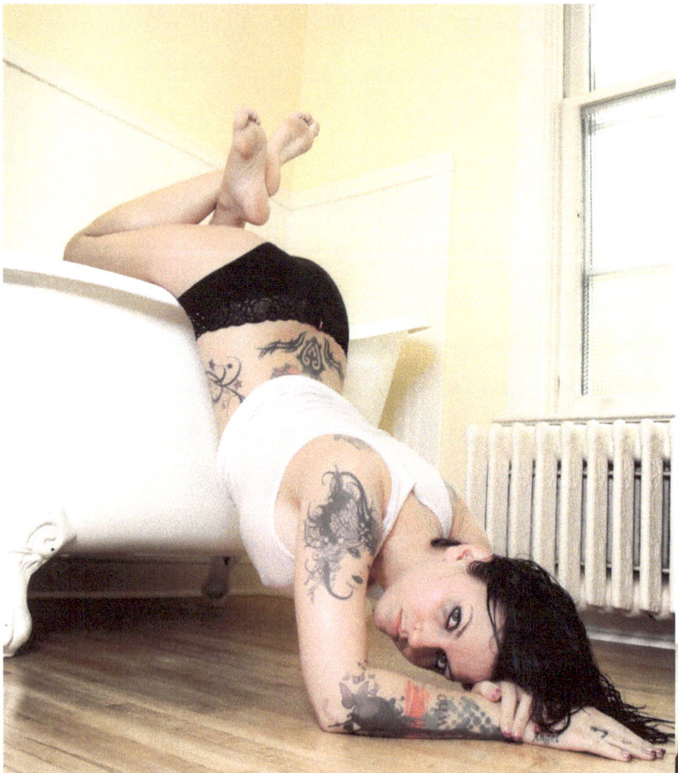

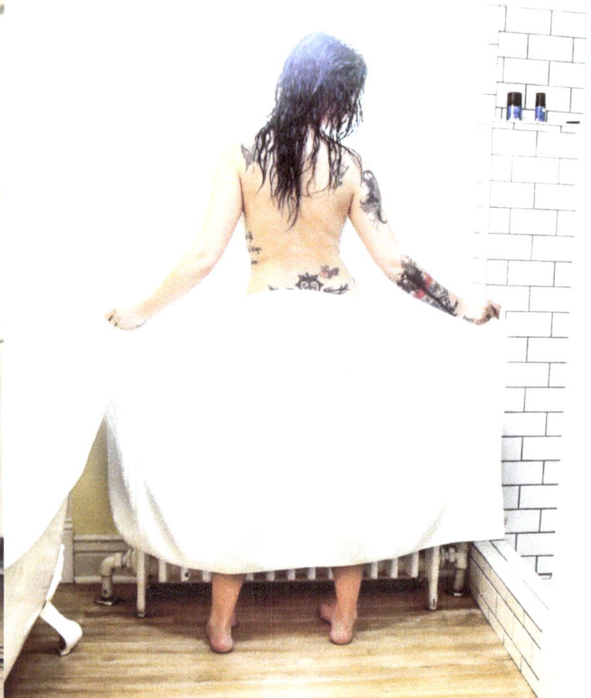

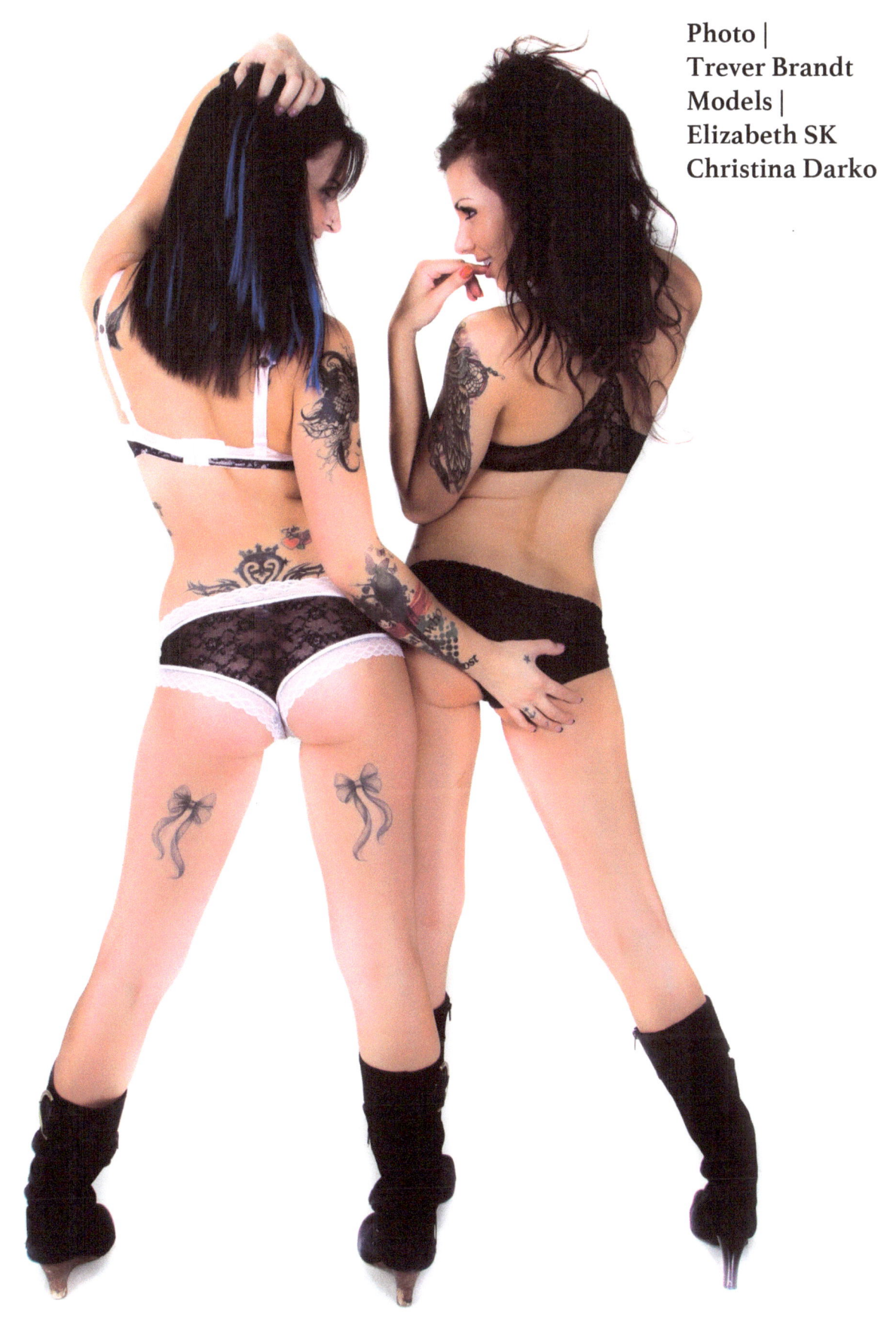

Photo |
Trever Brandt
Models |
Elizabeth SK
Christina Darko

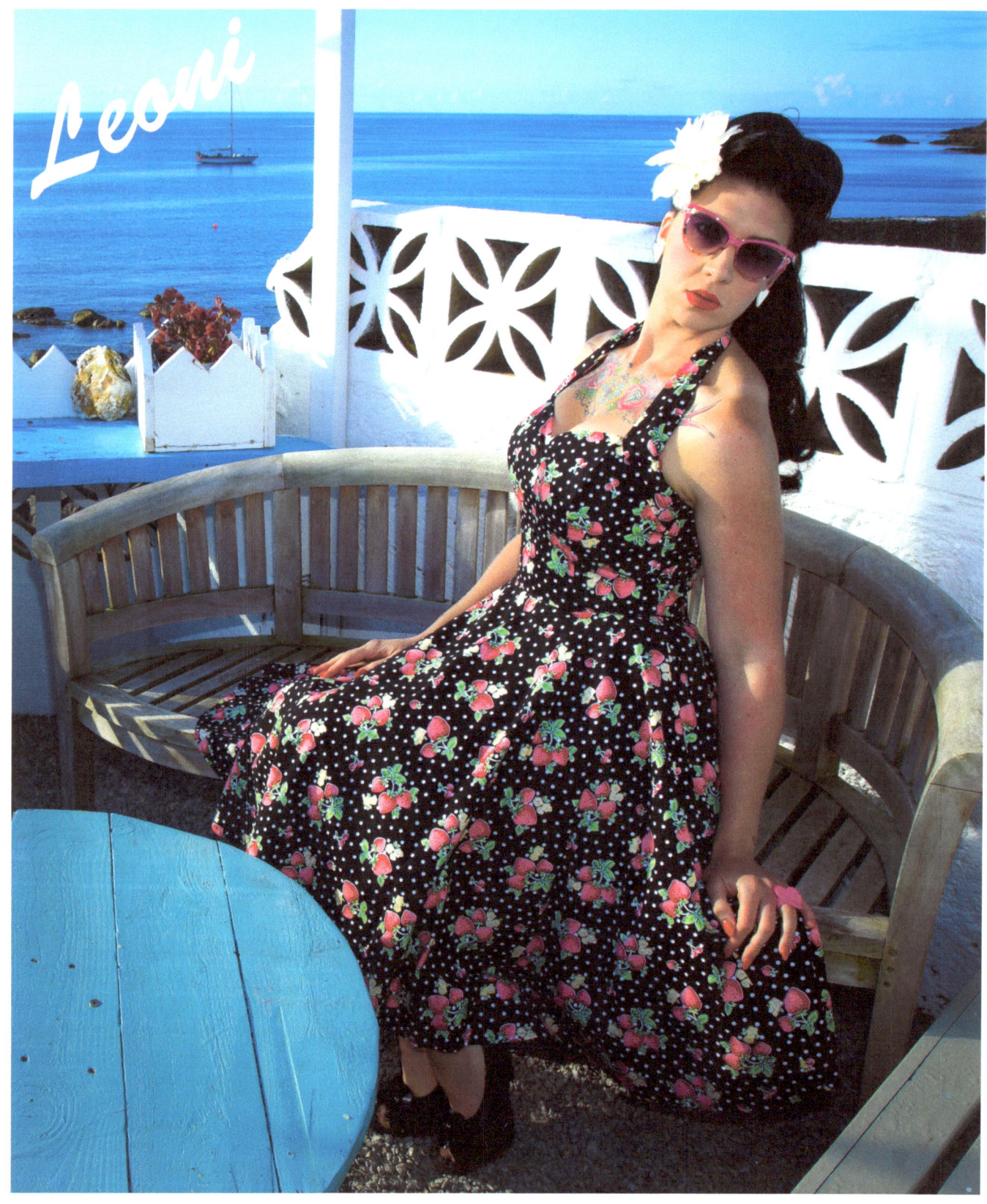

Model | Leoni IG @theliftingpinup
Photo | Lee Martin IG @commitbmx
Location | Mousehole, Cornwall, England

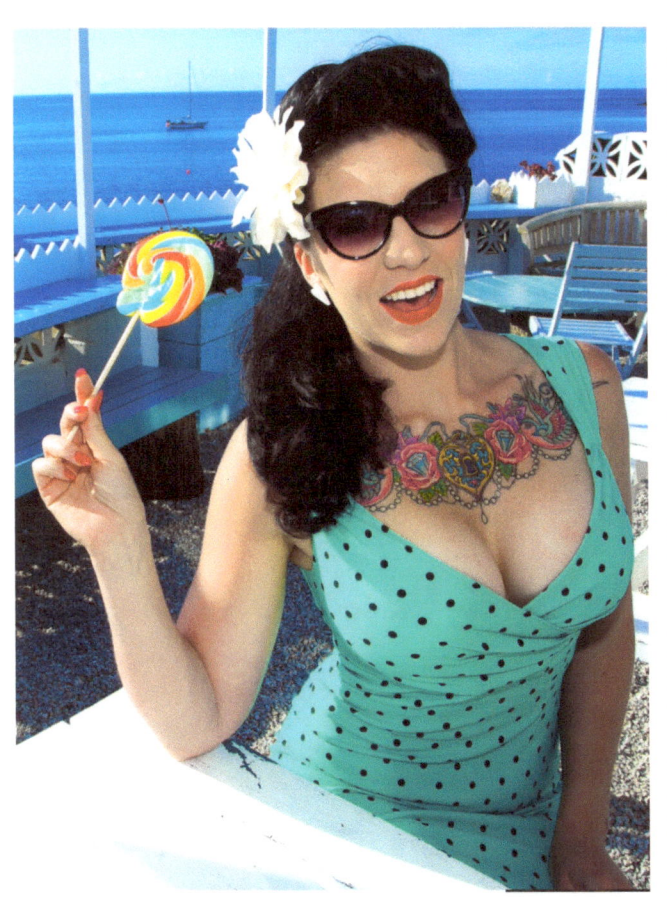
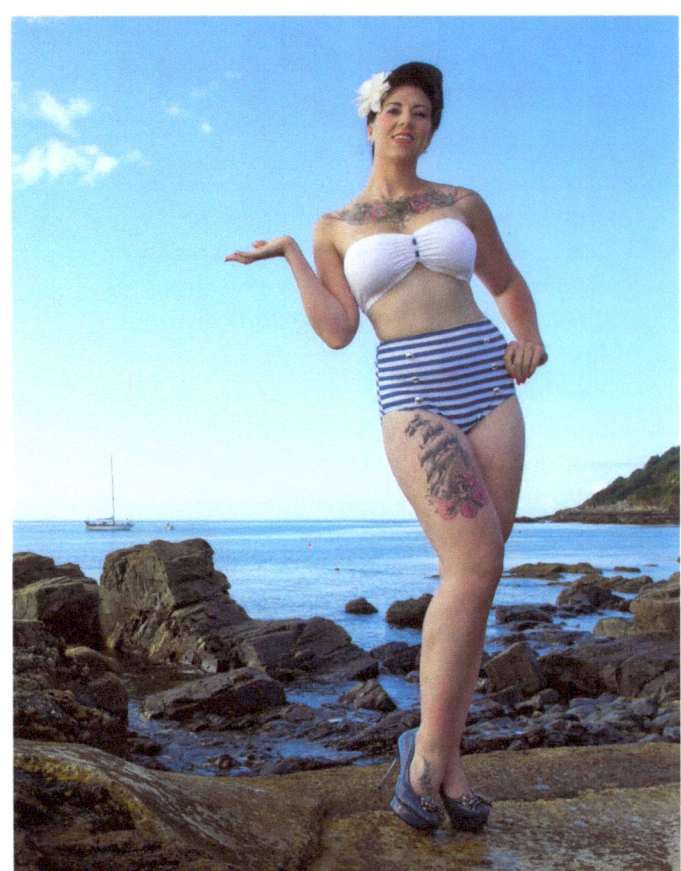

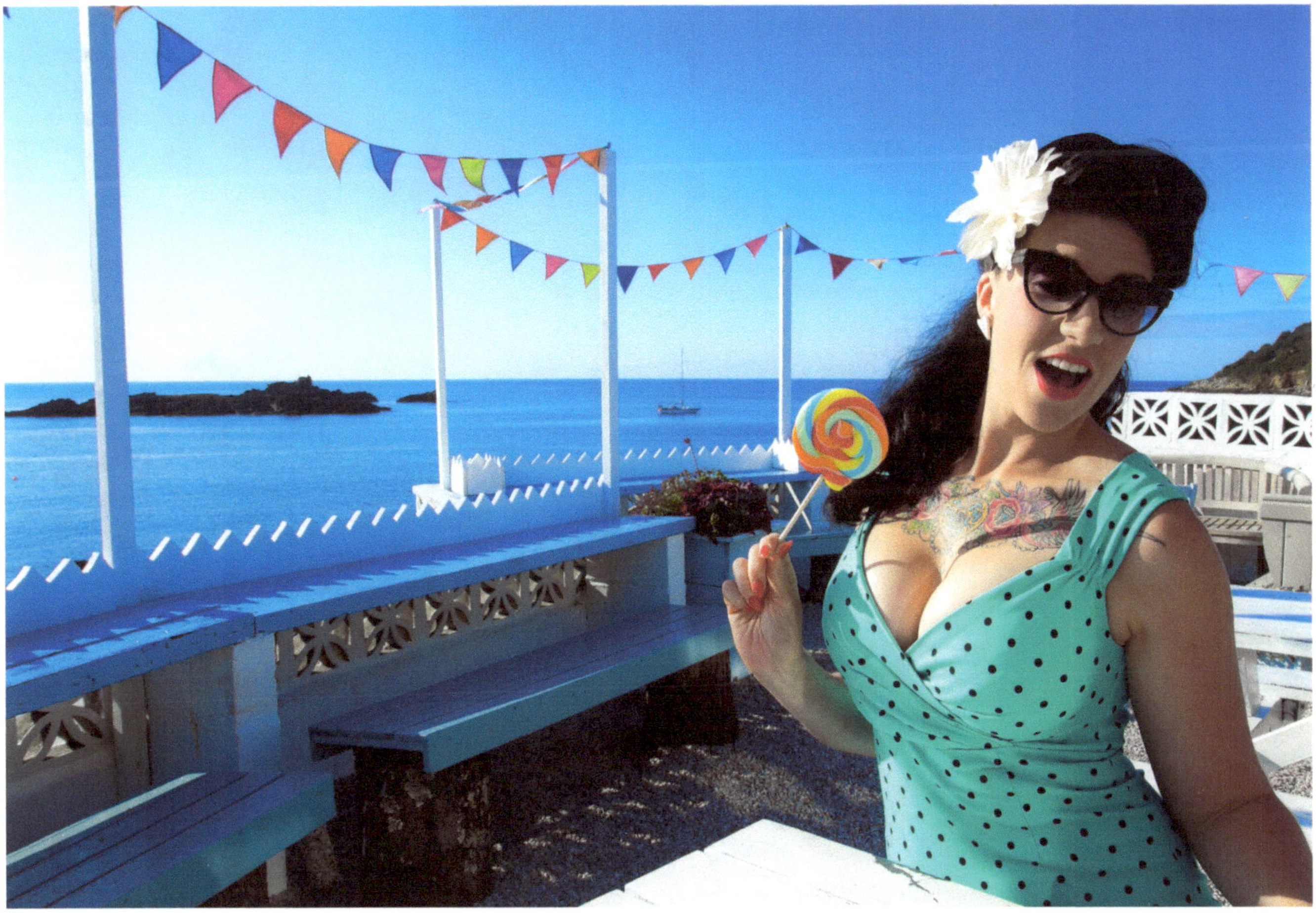

Julie Gems

Hey look everybody ! It's Julie Gems, the irresistible & intriguing femme fatale, equal parts old time glamour and modern day charm, let her tantalize you through the many diverse looks from American pinup photography from classic cheesecake to vintage bondage and couture fetish fashion from this modern day pinup.

"I like to create art through my photos using elements of classic iconic eras infused with my passion for surrealism and daring edge fashion, I feel the juxtaposition of the two elements makes for a more interesting photograph, I always try to involve all the elements of the photo for it's not always about the model that creates the art," says Julie Gems. You can see more of her portfolio on her website www.juliegems.com and Facebook page @ Julie Gems also on Instagram @ pinupjuliegems

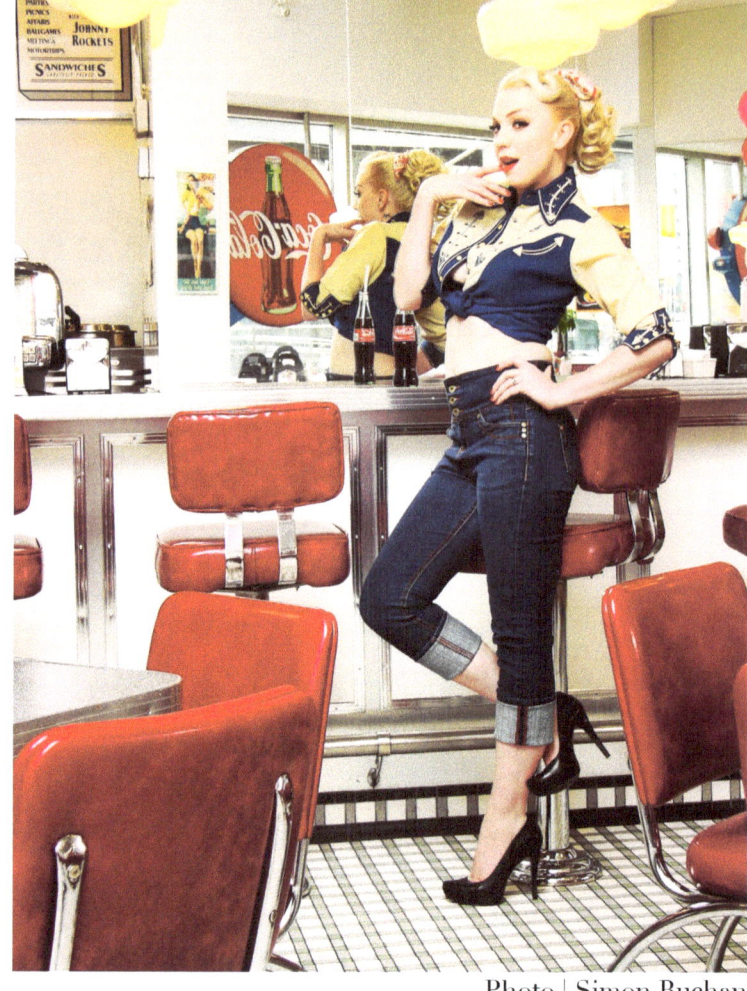

Photo | Simon Buchan

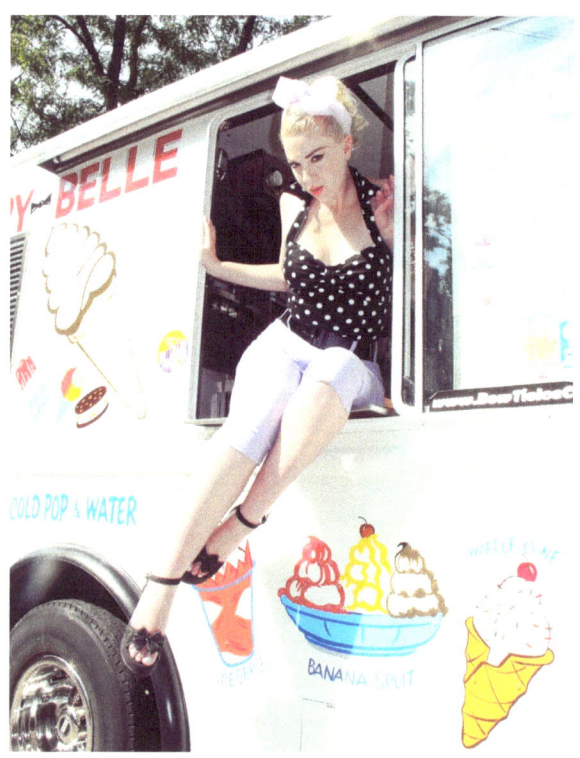

Clothing | Pinupgirlclothing

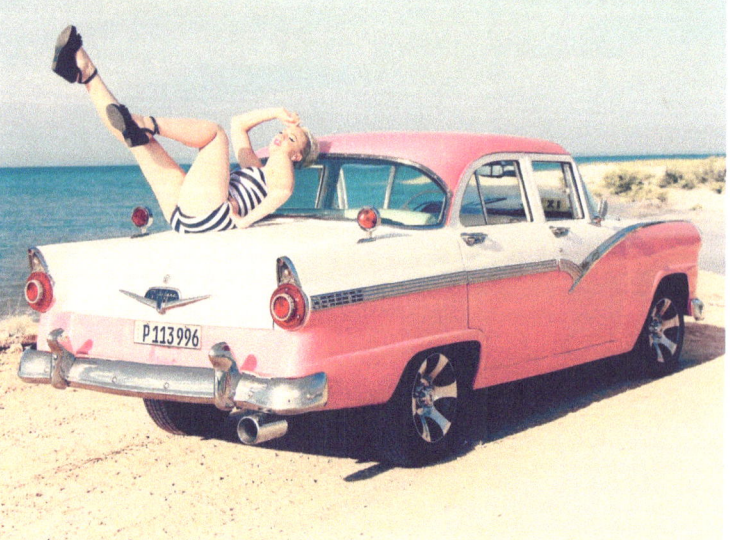

Clothing | Pop Swimsuits

Hair and Makeup by Julie Gems
Photos by Danny .D.
except for "5o's Diner" shot by Simon Buchan

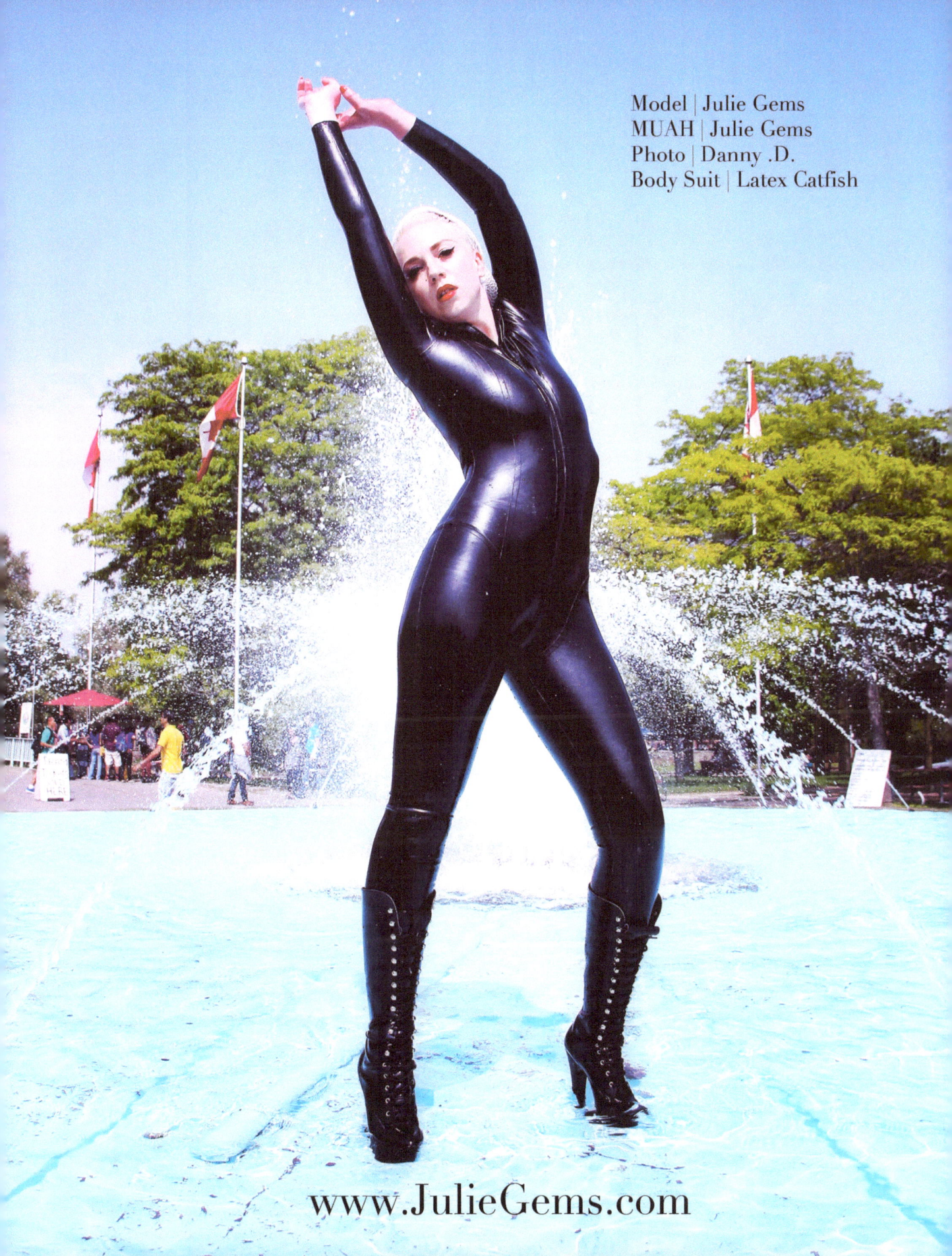

Model | Julie Gems
MUAH | Julie Gems
Photo | Danny .D.
Body Suit | Latex Catfish

www.JulieGems.com

Lynda Von Lotta

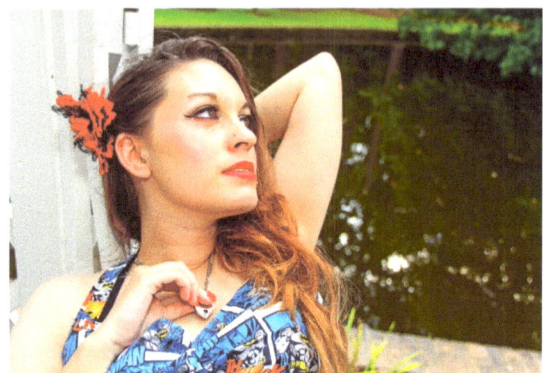

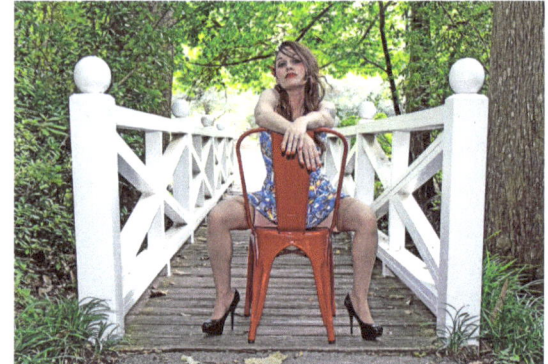

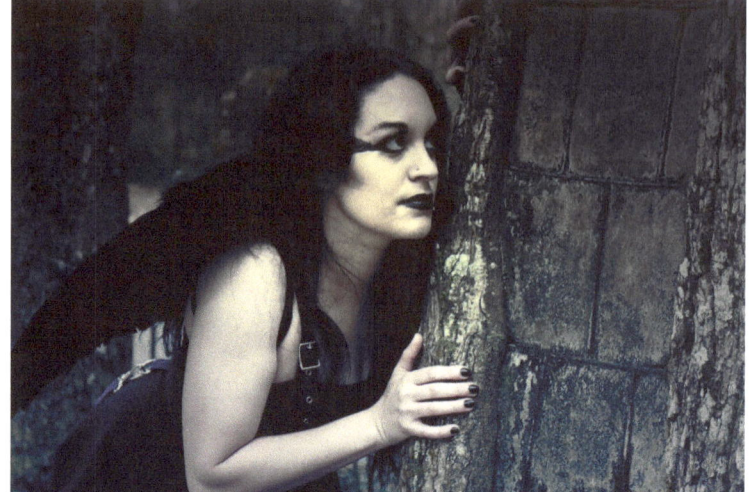

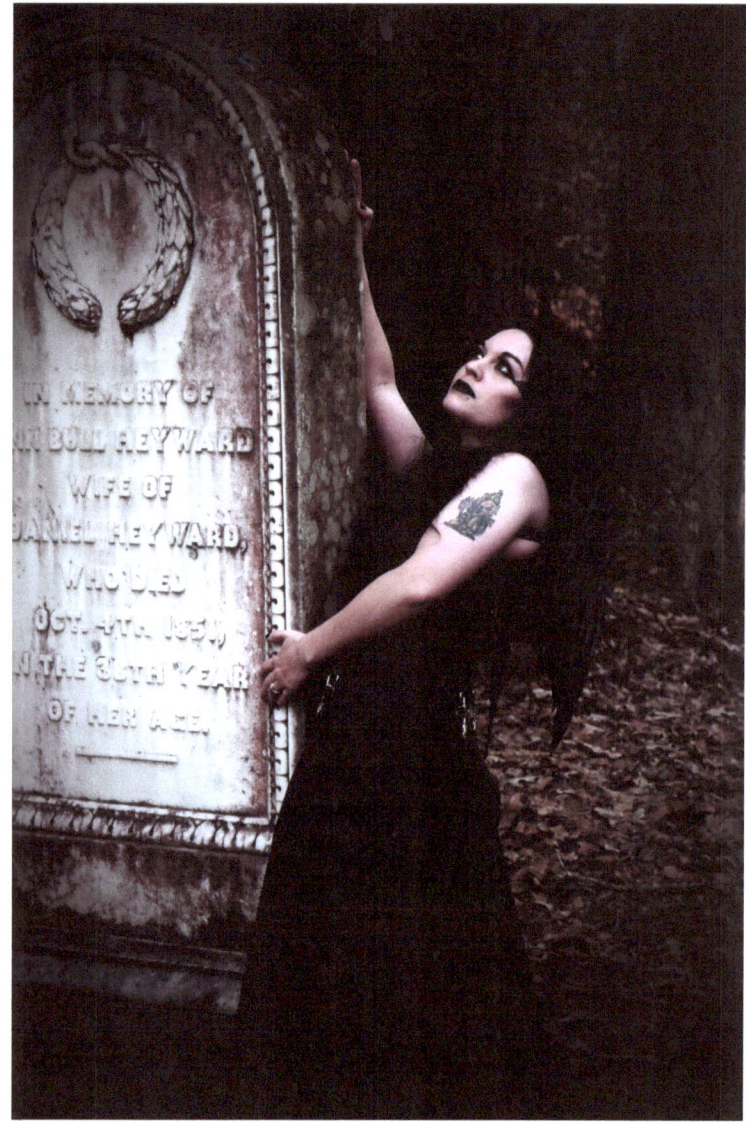

Model : Lynda Von Lotta
www.facebook.com/modelLyndaVonLotta
MUAH : Lynda Von Lotta
Photographer : Peter Von Egmond
Owner of One Sweet World Photo
facebook.com/pages/One-Sweet-World-Photo
Dress : Rebecca's Dorky Designs
facebook.com/RebeccasDorkyDesigns
Necklace : Ghostlove.com
facebook.com/GhostloveJewelry

"Fallen Angel"
Model : Lynda Von Lotta
Muah : Michelle Rose
www.facebook.com/michellerosedesigns
Photographer : Carol Donnelly
owner of Mad World Photo Imaging
www.facebook.com/madworldimaging

"Curiouser and Curiouser!"
Down the Rabbit Hole with Summer Rain

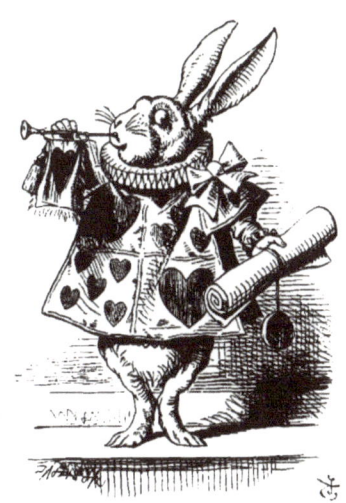

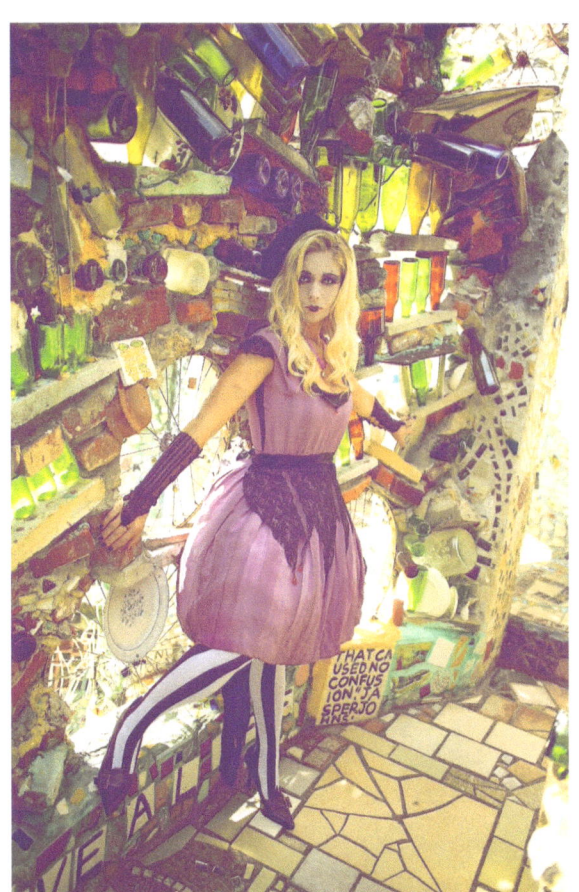

Model | Summer Rain
IG @s.rain14
Photos | Limelight Boudoir
www.facebook.com/limelightboudoir
Philadelphia, Pennsylvania

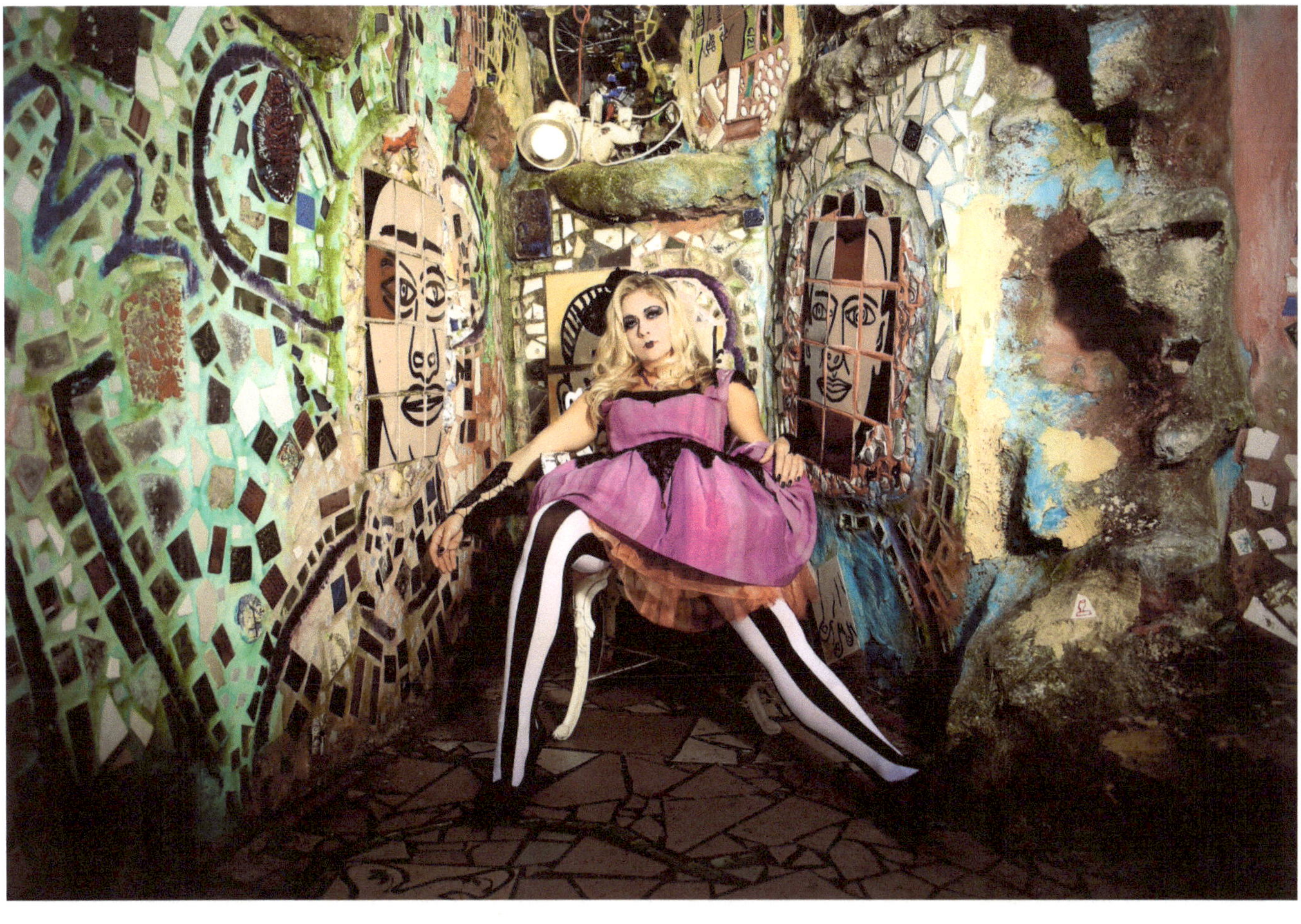

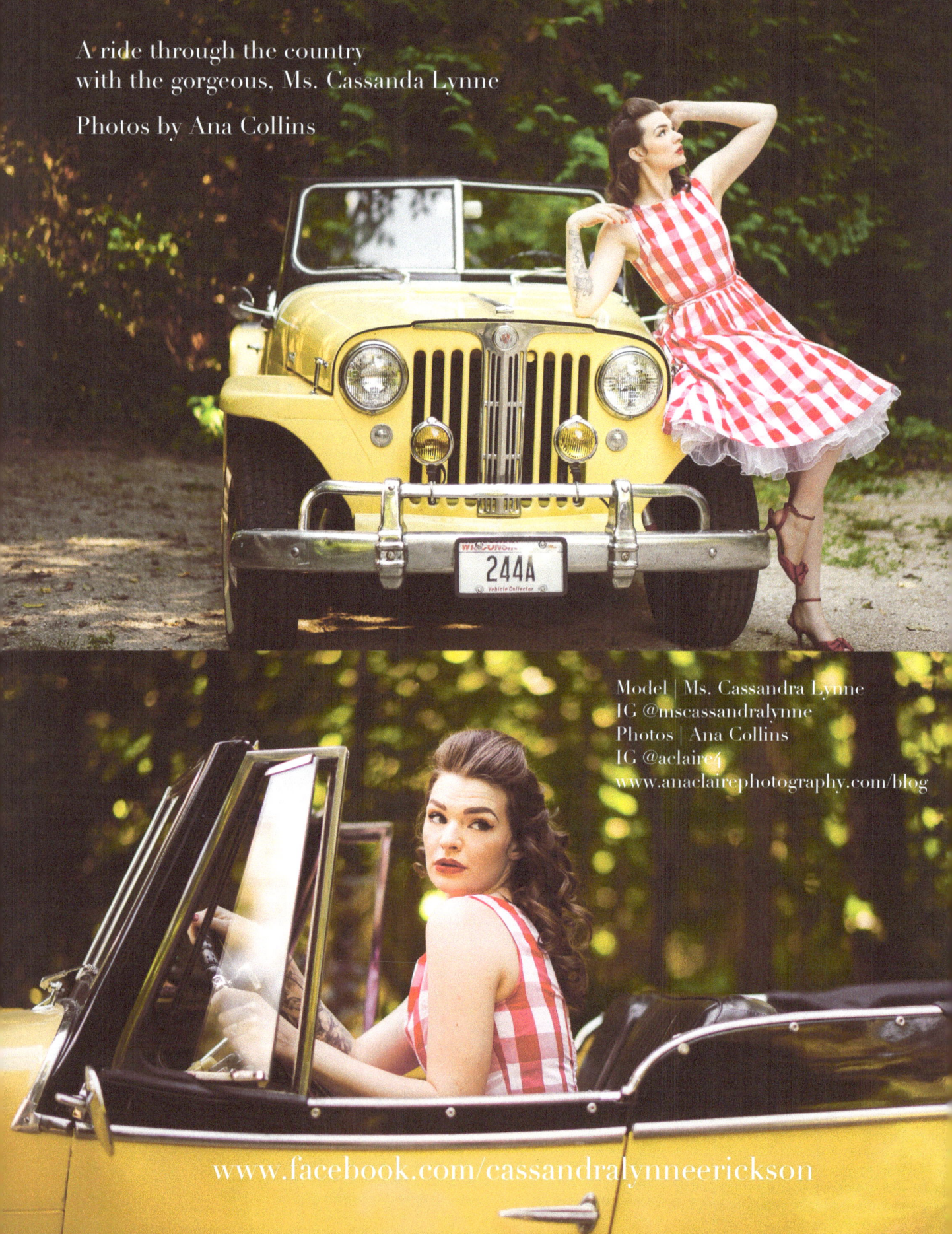

A ride through the country
with the gorgeous, Ms. Cassanda Lynne

Photos by Ana Collins

Model | Ms. Cassandra Lynne
IG @mscassandralynne
Photos | Ana Collins
IG @aclaire4
www.anaclairephotography.com/blog

www.facebook.com/cassandralynneerickson

Ms. Cassandra Lynne is a little lady with a big heart and Midwestern charm. A stay at home mother of two young boys, Cassandra works as a freelance writer and model supporting progressive politics and charitable causes.

Showing a passion for photography and modeling at an early age, Cassandra spent hours mesmerized by photographs of her late Grandmother Madeline, who began her modeling career as a young girl during the Great Depression. For a time, it was Madeline's income that solely supported herself as well as her two sisters and parents.

A believer in magic and the power of love, Cassandra is presently studying to become a philosopher of metaphysical studies. As an interfaith priestess, Cassandra spends her days honoring and studying all forms of religion, spirituality and faith across all walks of life. Finding magnificent reward as a spiritual counselor and a local teacher of ritual design and spiritual symbolism, she still takes no greater joy than when given the honor to bless the union of two people in love.

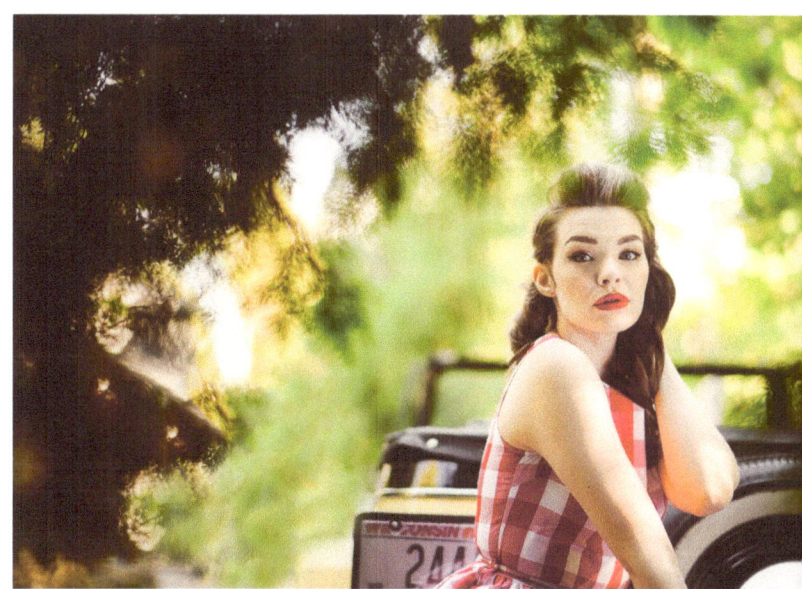

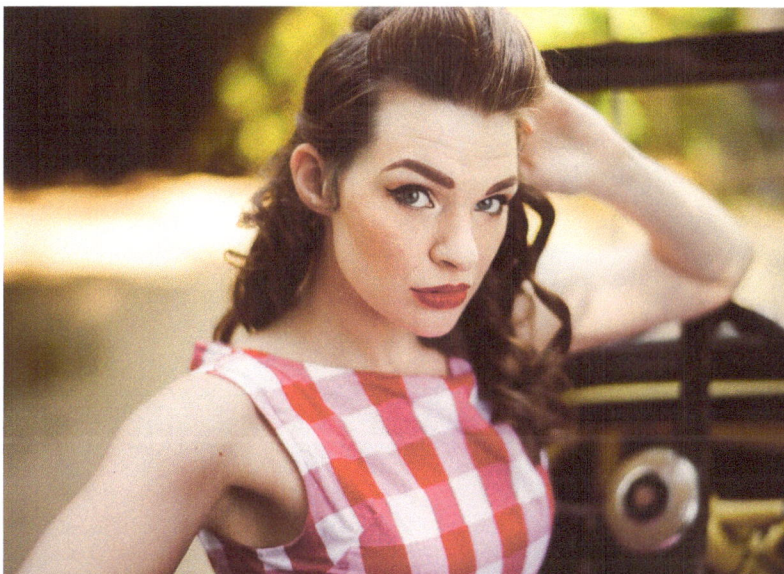

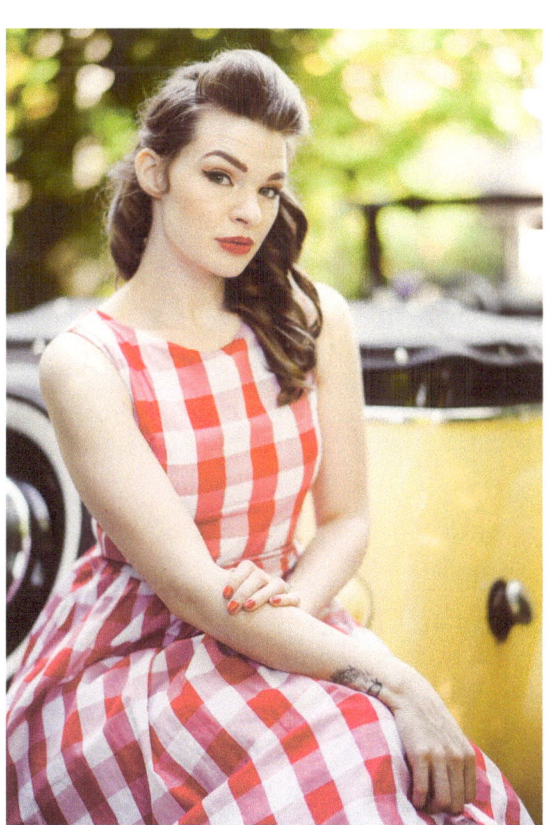

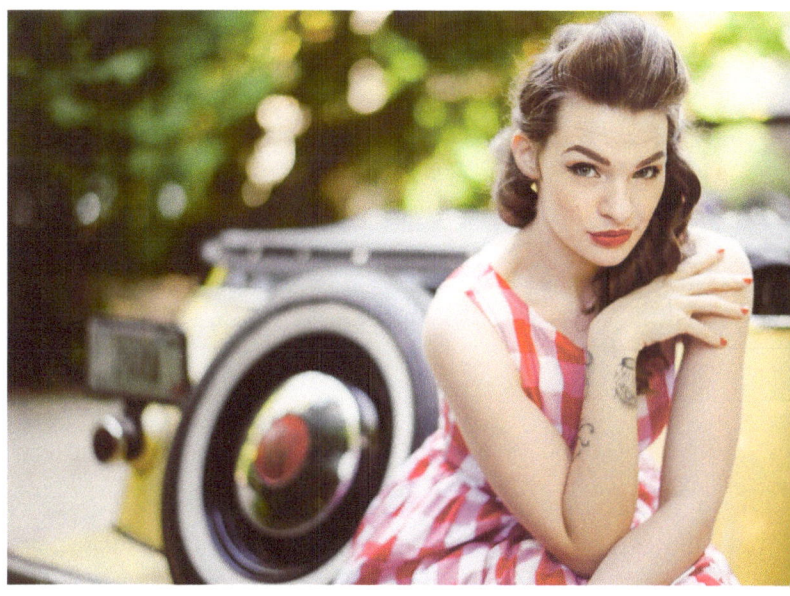

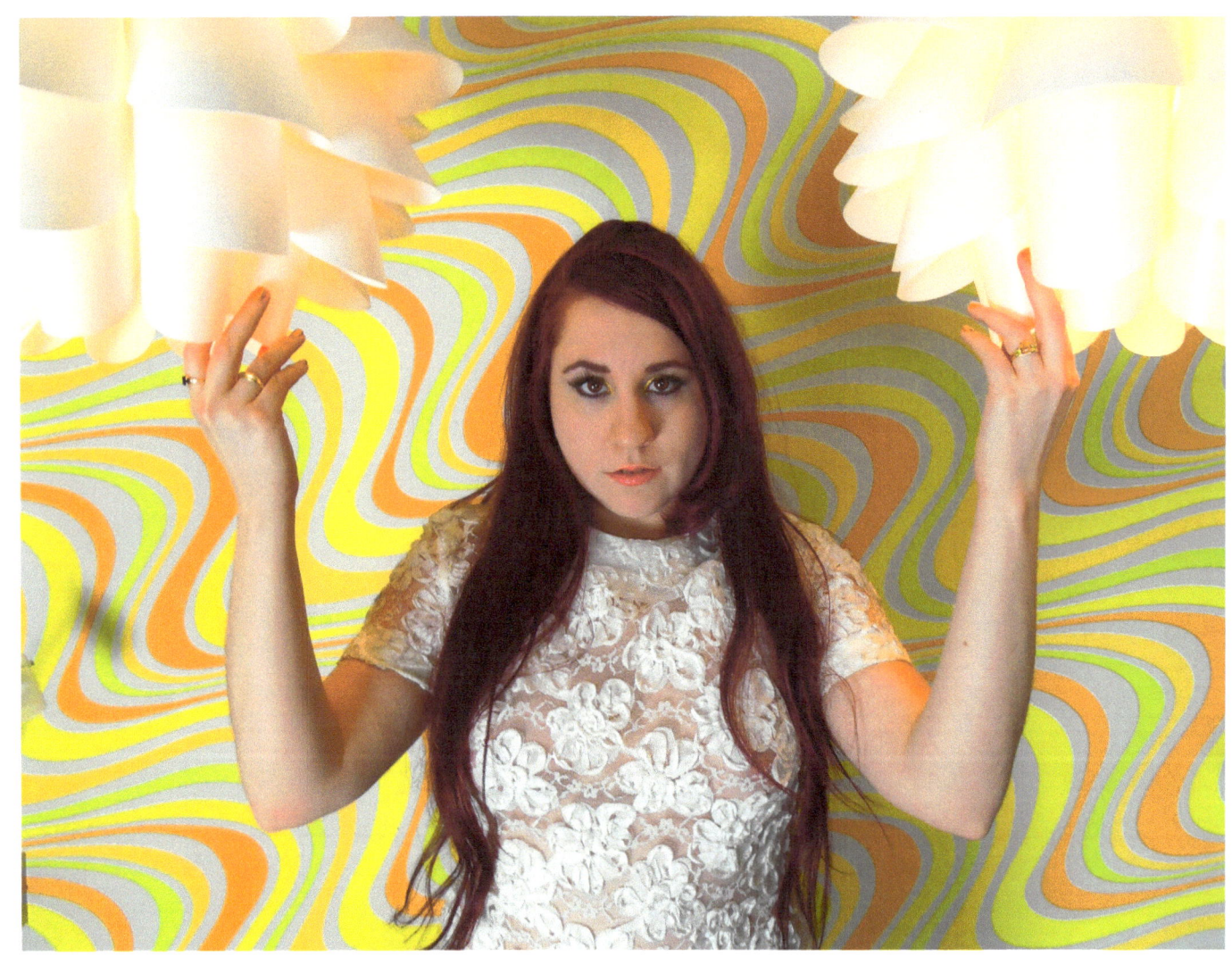

Model | Nissa Citrine
www.facebook.com/NissaJeanCitrine
Photo | Wild Earp Photography
www.facebook.com/wild.earp.photography

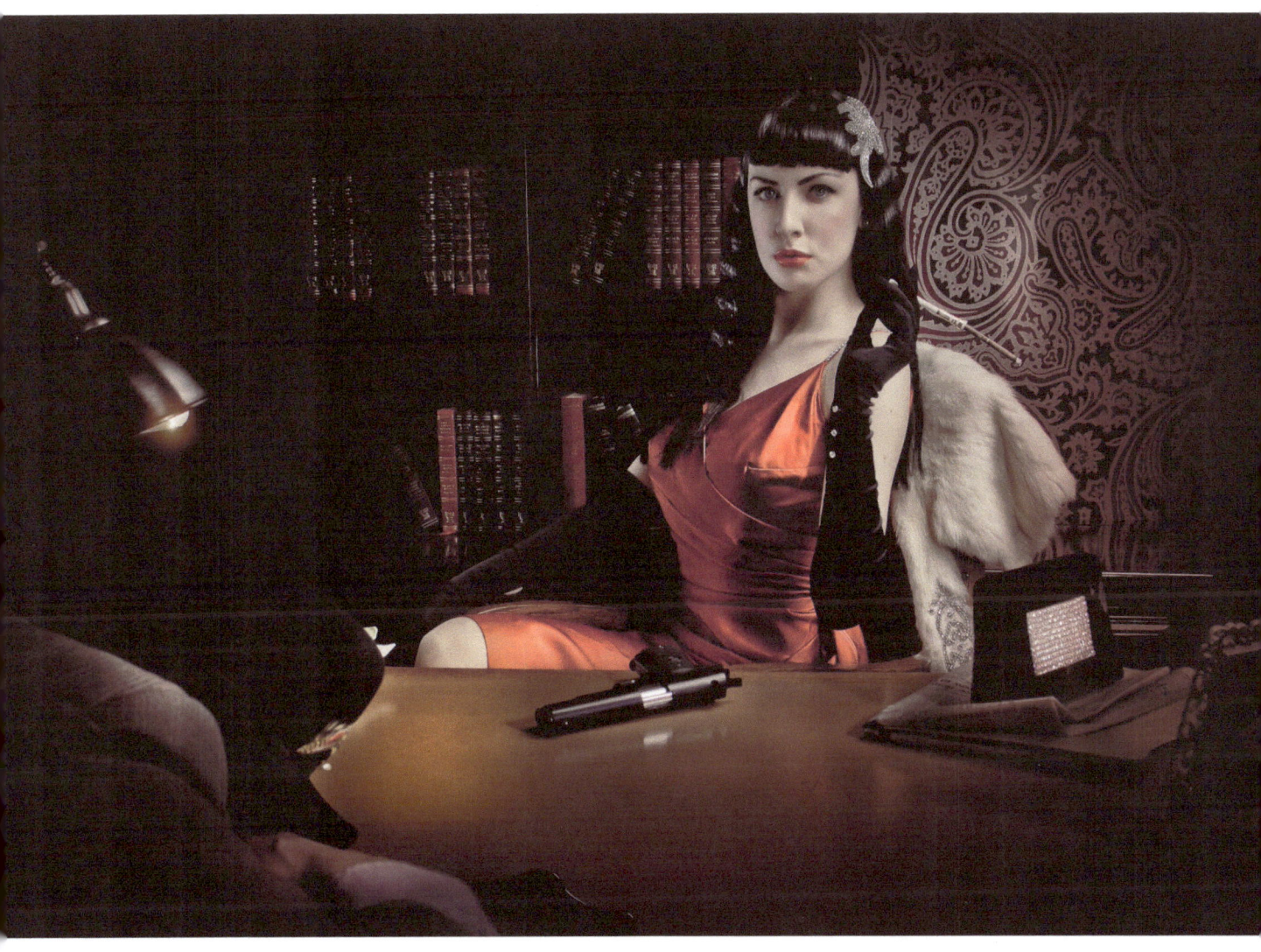

Model/MUA: Black Swan Persona\
www.facebook.com/BlackSwanPersonaModel
Instagram @blackswanpersona
Photographer: Don't Shoot Me Photography
Wardrobe: Dirty Fabulous Vintage Clothing

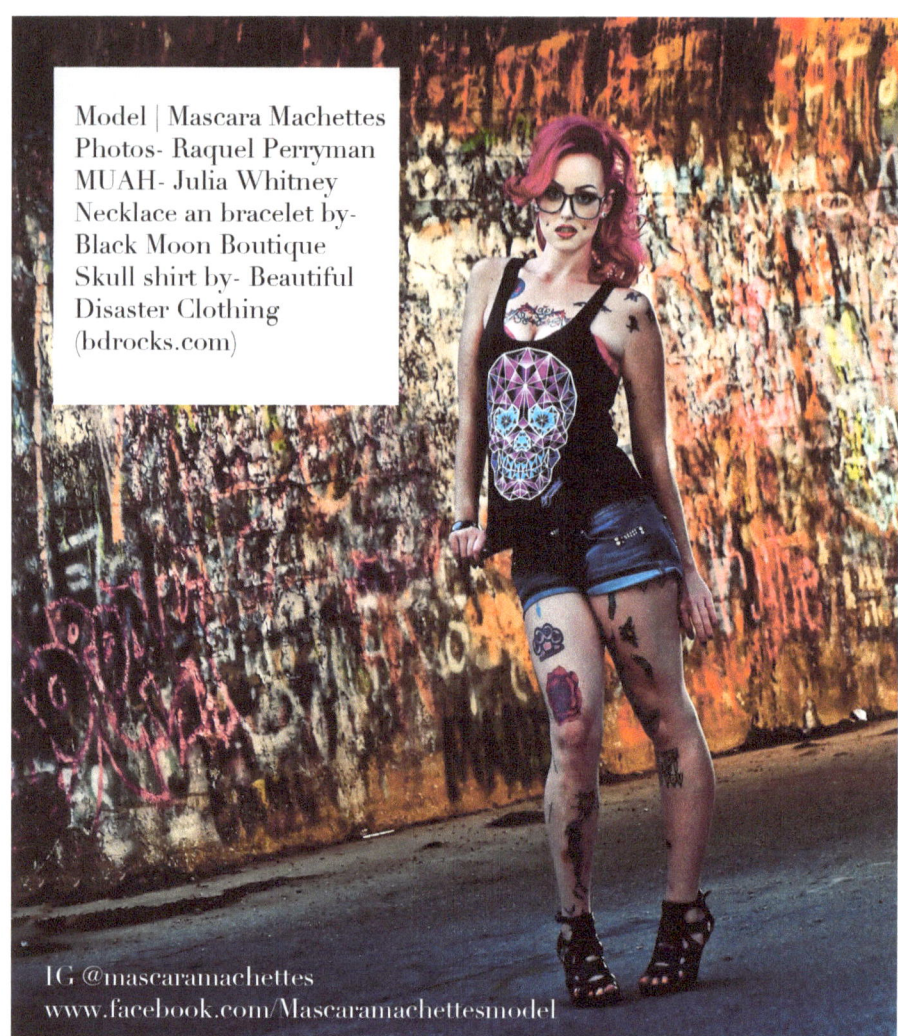

Model | Mascara Machettes
Photos- Raquel Perryman
MUAH- Julia Whitney
Necklace an bracelet by-
Black Moon Boutique
Skull shirt by- Beautiful
Disaster Clothing
(bdrocks.com)

IG @mascaramachettes
www.facebook.com/Mascaramachettesmodel

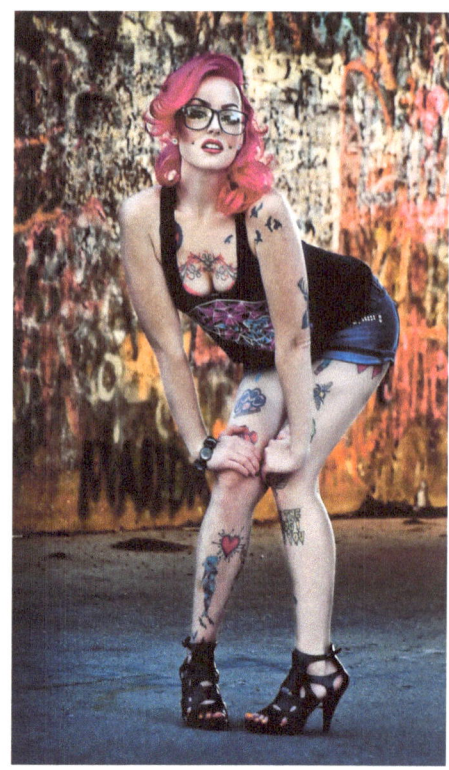

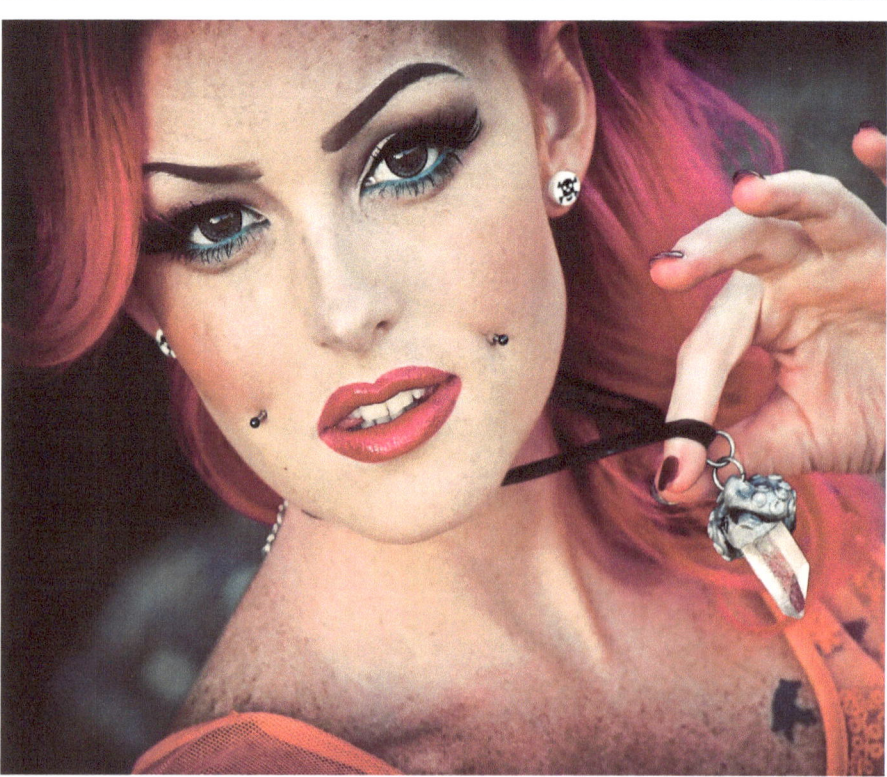

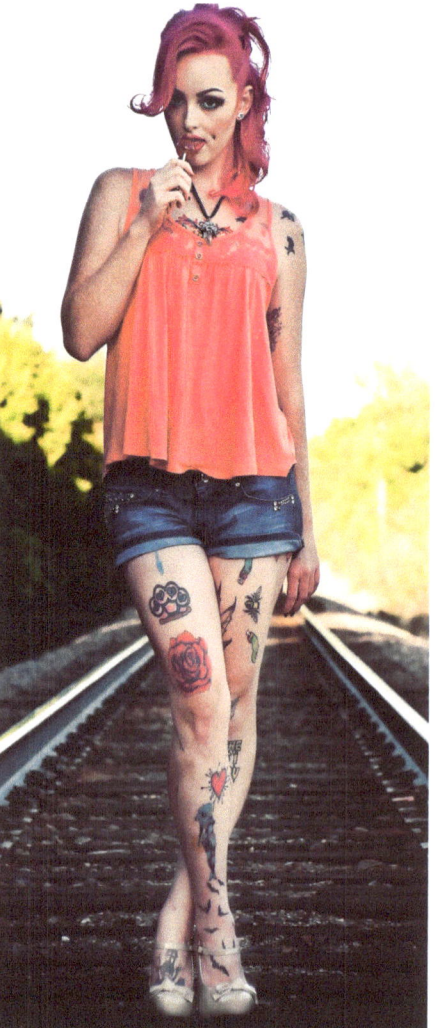

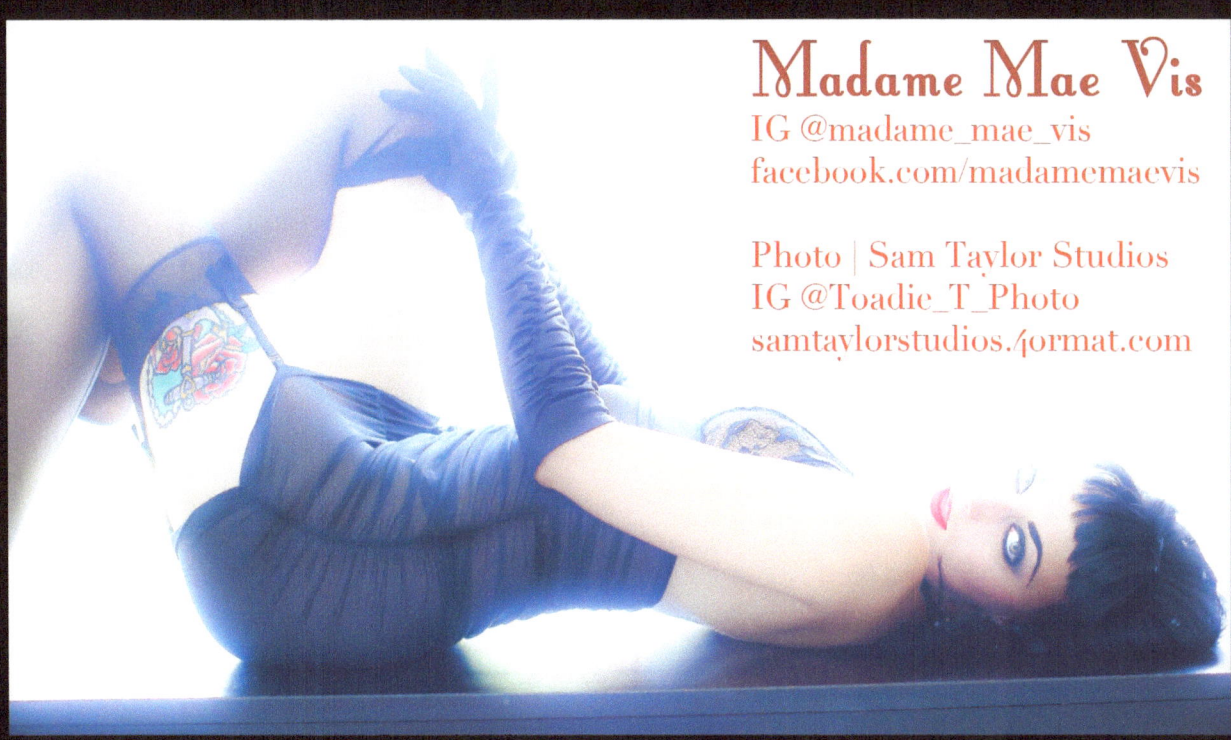

Madame Mae Vis

IG @madame_mae_vis
facebook.com/madamemaevis

Photo | Sam Taylor Studios
IG @Toadie_T_Photo
samtaylorstudios.4ormat.com

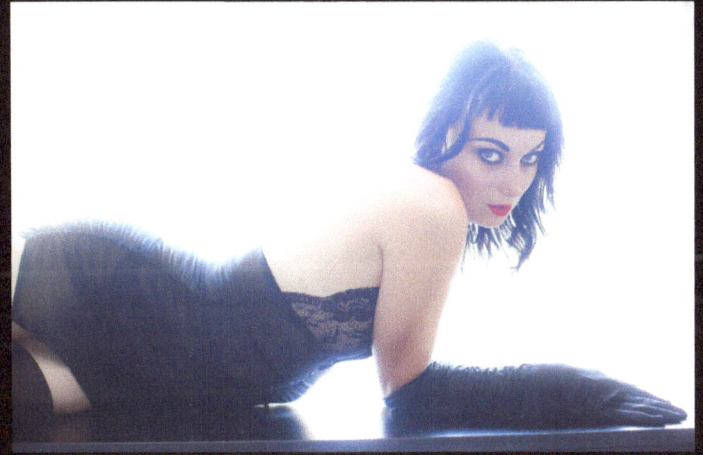

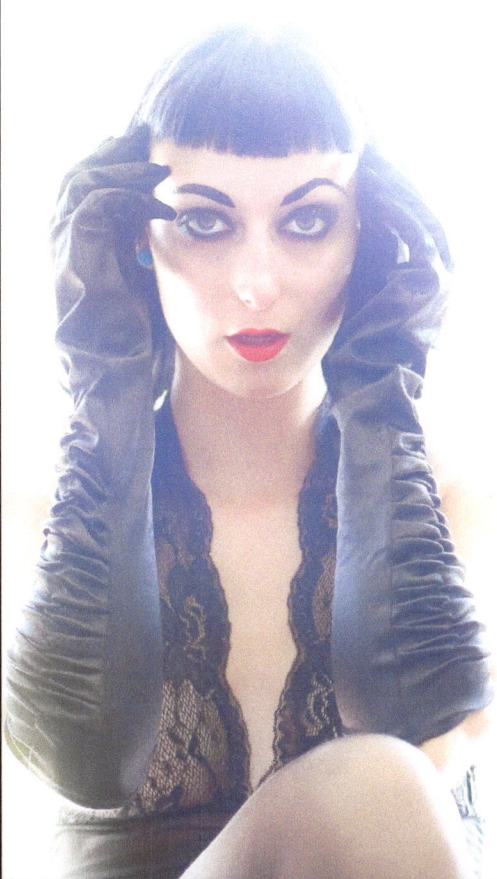

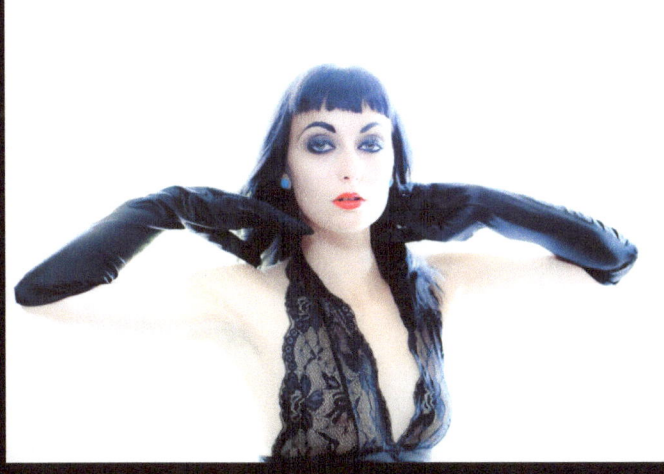

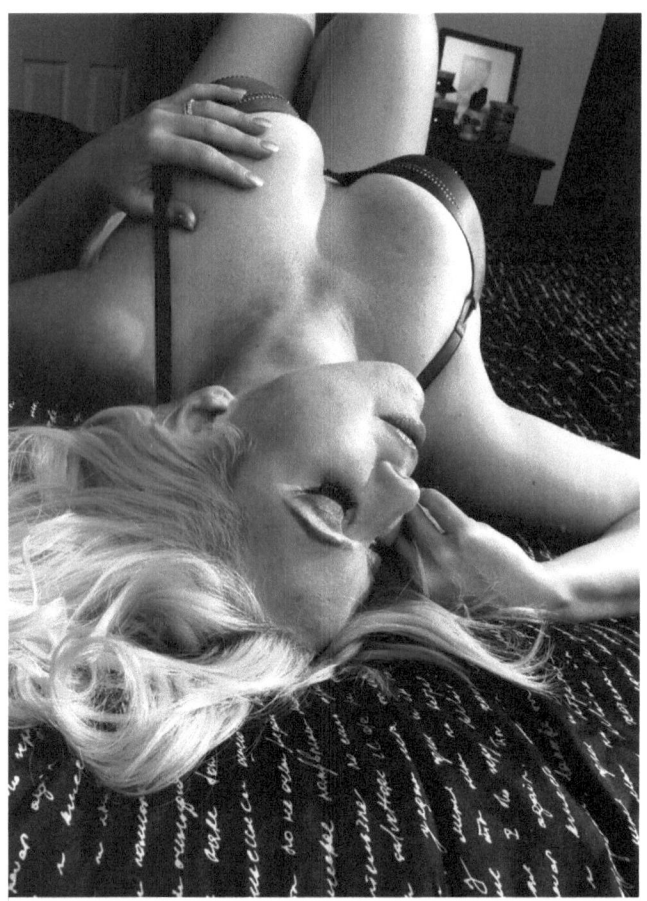

Model | Contessa
IG @curvy_doll13
Photo | Ashley Lim
IG @sunkissedexposures
MUAH | Mirna Iliana
IG @makeupartistrybymirna

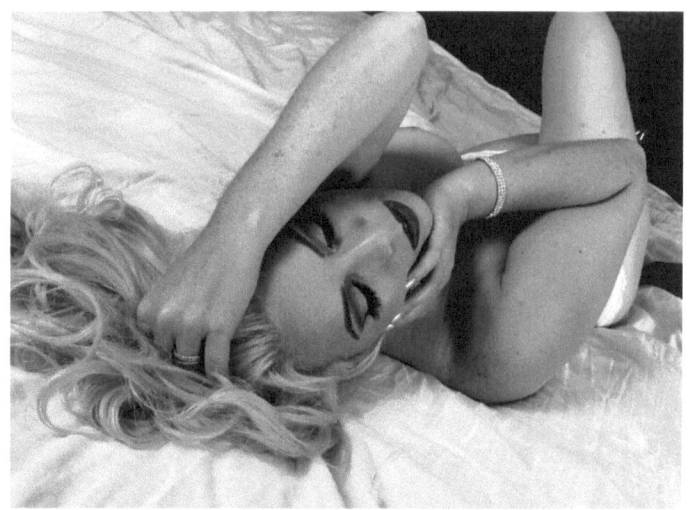

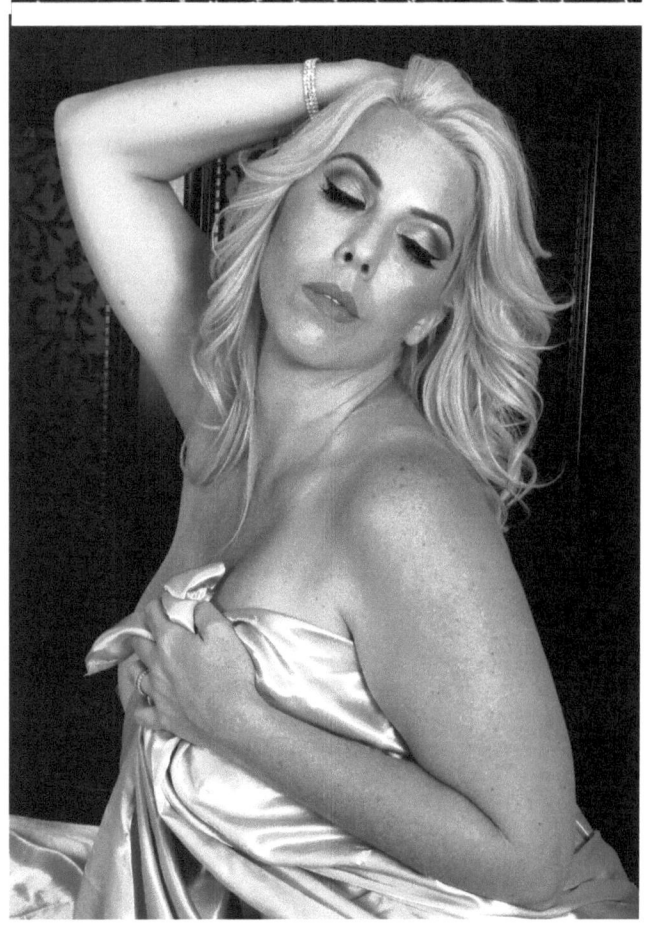

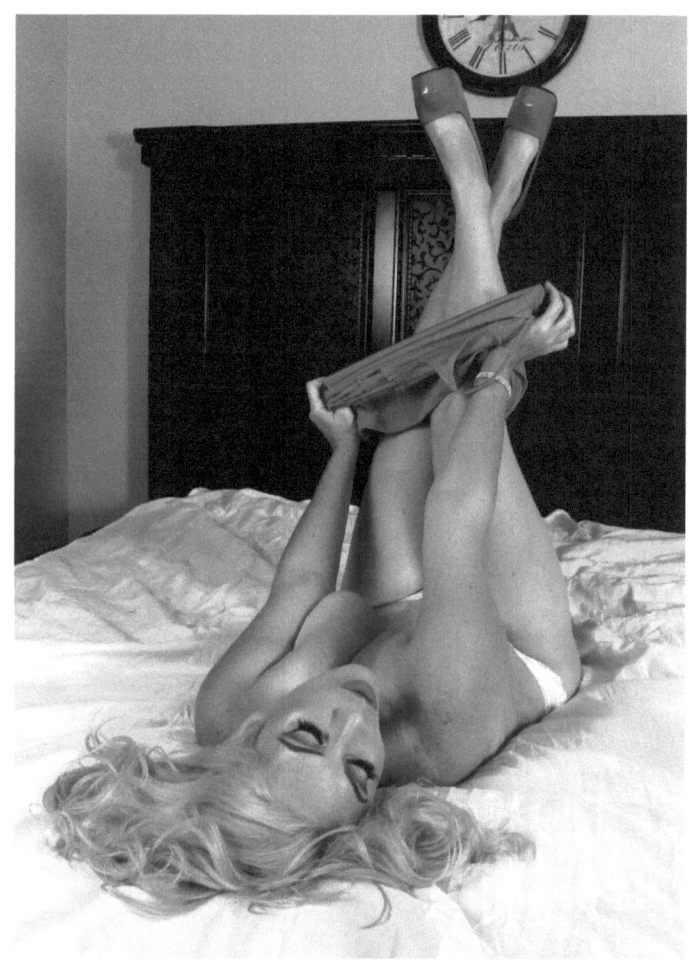

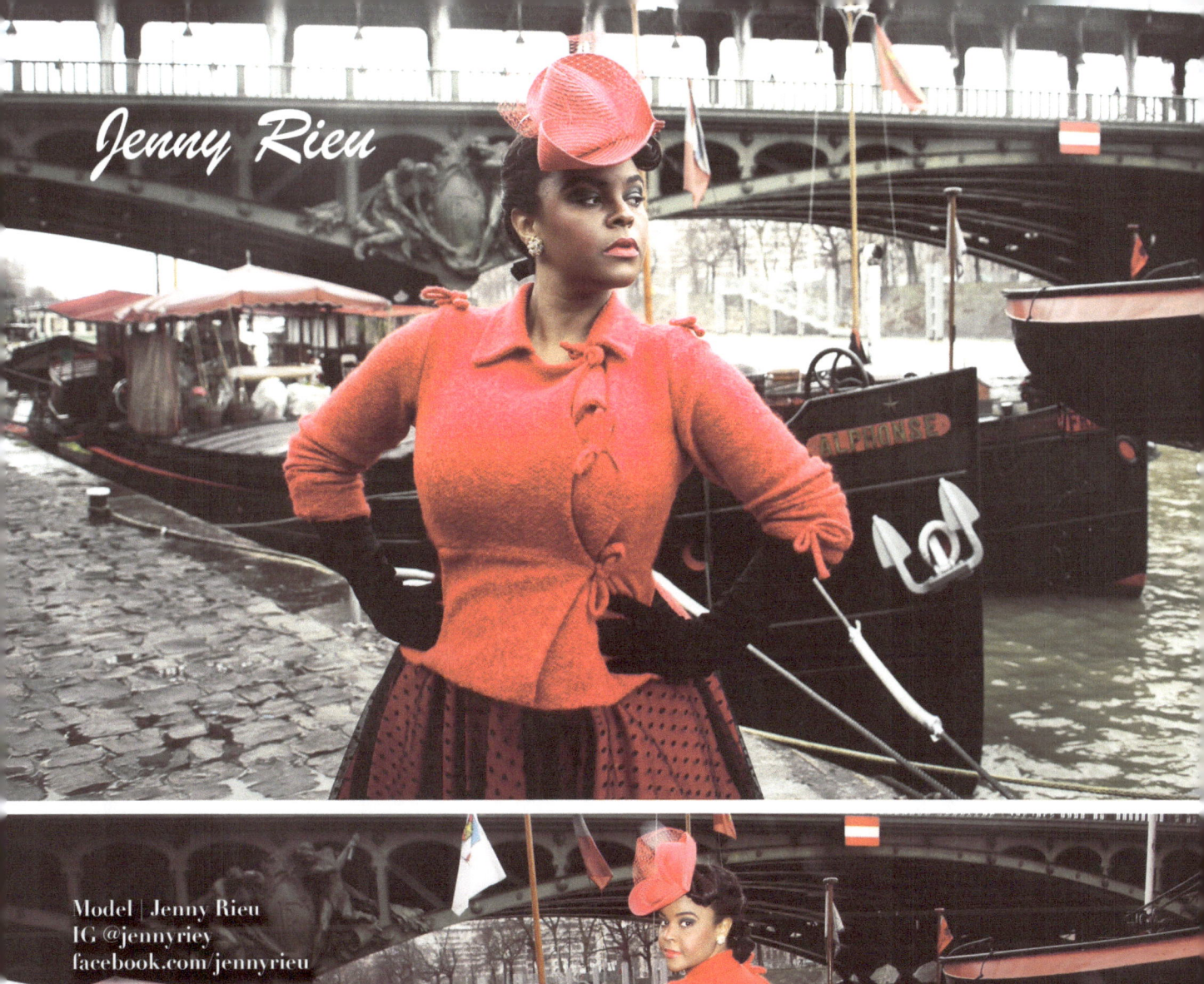

Jenny Rieu

Model | Jenny Rieu
IG @jennyriey
facebook.com/jennyrieu

MUAH | Styling | Jenny Rieu

Photo | Jason Kamimura
IG @jason_kamimura_photography
facebook.com/jasonkamimuraphotography

Hat | Jessika Hill Couture Millinery
www.jessikahill.com

Dress | Pinup Girl Clothing
www.PinupGirlClothing.com

Cardigan | Antoine Et Lili
www.antoineetlili.com

Location | Pont de Bir-Hakeim, Paris

VON SWEETS

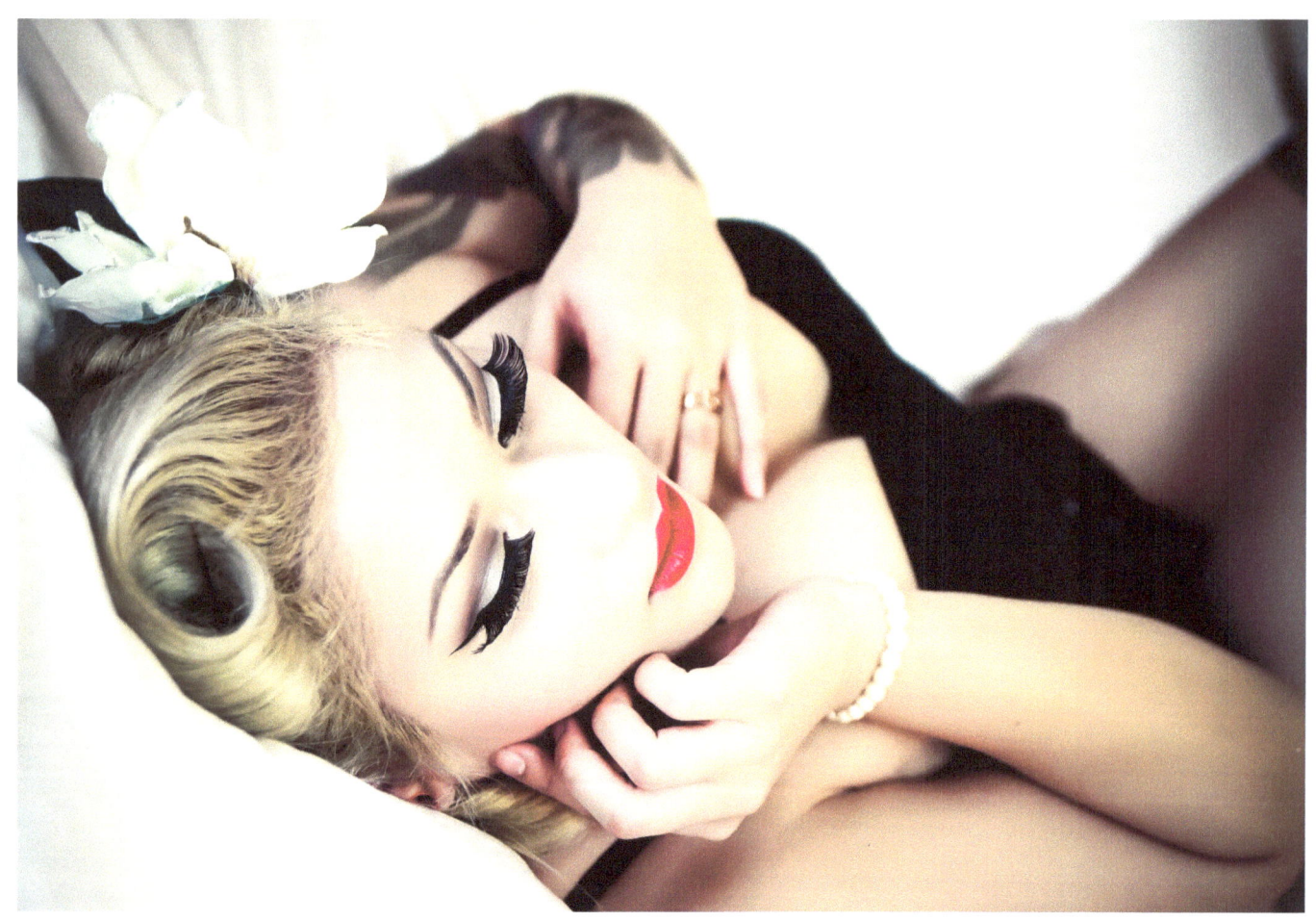

Model | MUAH :Von Sweets

Photo | Celebrate Your Sexy

Hair Flower | Niccococreations

Instagram @ari.barbie

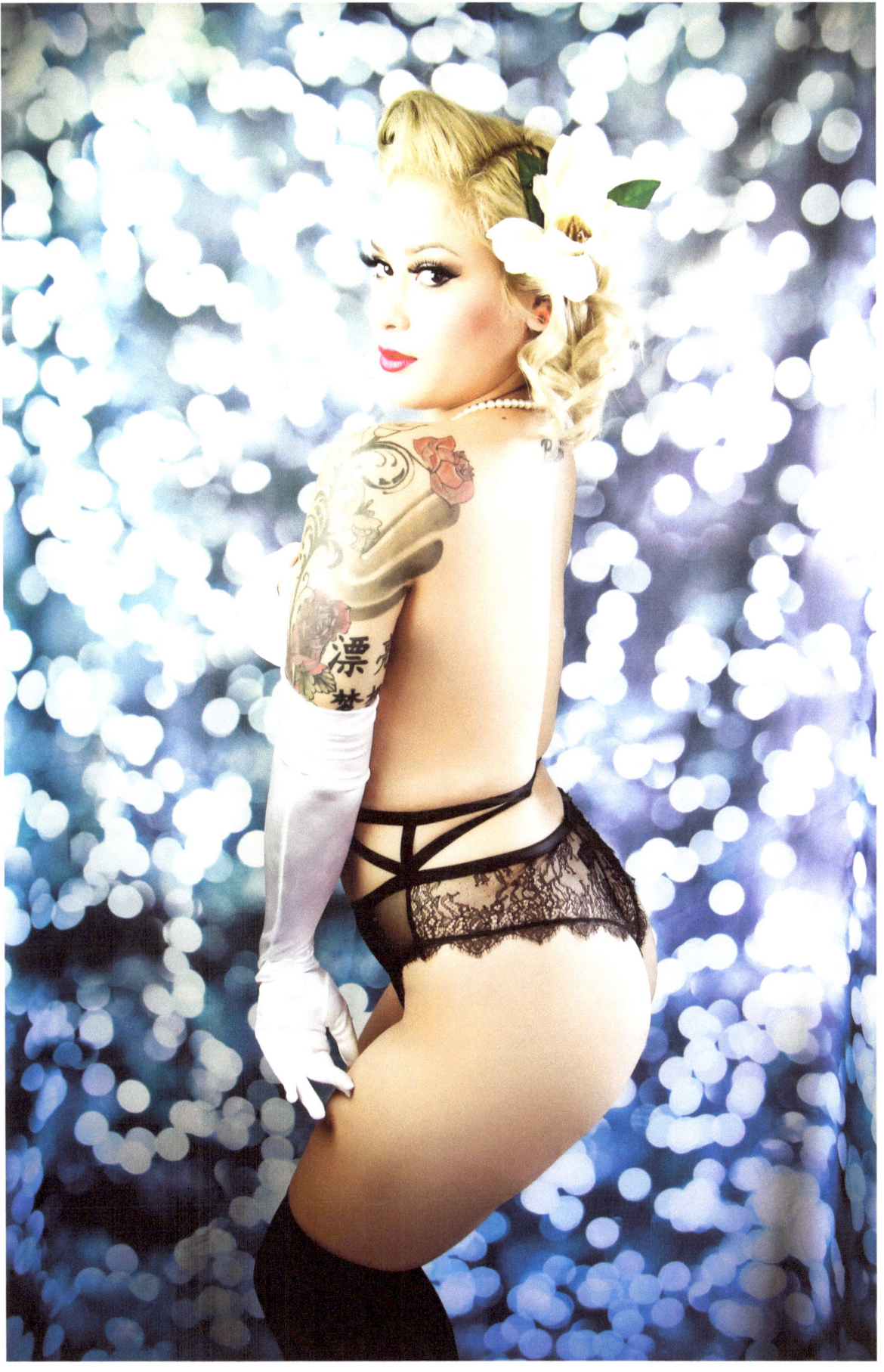

We hope you enjoyed Pinup Alternative Issue 1. Thank you for all of your support. Coming soon look for the "Special Saucy" Issue showcasing artistic nudes and sexy lingerie. Here's a sneak peek for now featuring Internatianally acclaimed burlesque star Sandria Dore'.

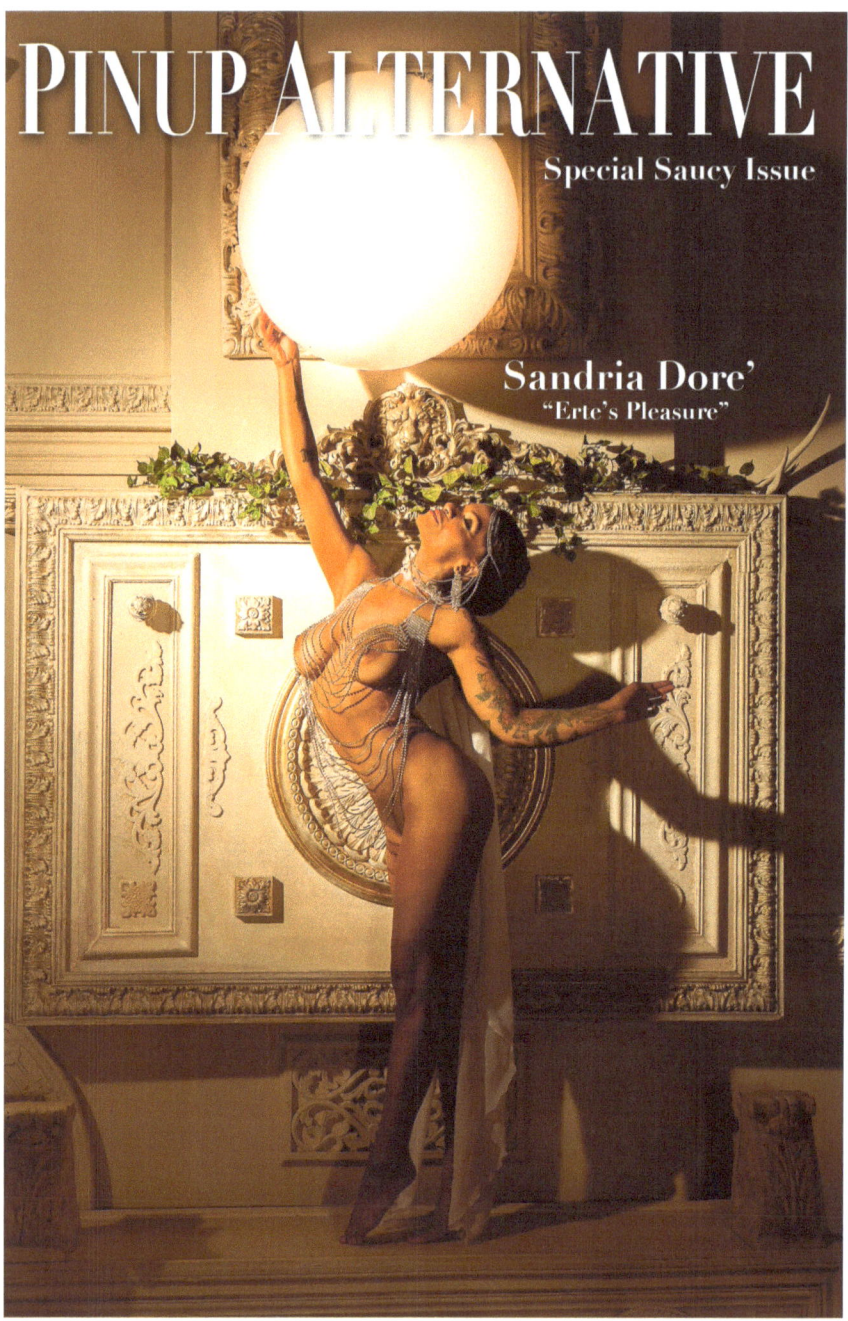

Model: Sandria Dore'
Photographed By: Double L Photography
Set Design: Julian James Wilde
Styling: Melissa Grant
Body Chain: DuBarry Fashion LVNV
Shot at: The Machine

www.ingramcontent.com/pod-product-compliance
Lightning Source LLC
Chambersburg PA
CBHW050743180526
45159CB00003B/1326